TRIUMPH FROM TRAGEDY

PERSONAL STORIES OF STRUGGLE, COURAGE, HOPE, AND VICTORY

CHRISTIAN WRITERS FOR LIFE

Copyright © 2021 by Christian Writers for Life

All rights reserved.

No part of this book may be reproduced in any form or by any electronic or mechanical means, including information storage and retrieval systems, without written permission from the author, except for the use of brief quotations in a book review.

ISBN: 9798786933117

CONTENTS

Introduction	vii
1. The Shore By Donna Kay	1
2. Surgery at Thirteen Years Old By Linda Weaver Clarke	5
3. The Battle Belongs to God By Stephen D. Edwards	9
4. The "L" on My Forehead By Nancy Lee Bethea	13
5. Connecting in Difficult Times By Ruth "Reno" Anderson	17
6. Much Like Joseph By Desire Nana	21
7. God Knows By Wolfgang Bernhardt	25
8. Music—My Calling! By Lynne Drysdale Patterson	29
9. The Shipwreck By Teresa Newton-Terres	33
10. To Err Is Human By Linda Marie	37
11. God's Promises By Carolyn Kazmierczak	41
12. Time Waits for No One By Alberta Sequeira	45
13. Janetta, You Will Always Matter By Janetta Fudge Messmer	49
14. Saying Goodbye By Pam Waddell	51
15. I Hear Him By Cheryl Schuermann	55
16. If Only It Had Been Me By Stephanie Frelone	59
17. Frost in My Soul By Emma Bloor	63

18. The Secrets We Keep 67
    By Linda L. Kruschke
19. Rescued by an Angel 71
    By Cecilia James
20. Purposeful Pain 75
    By Susan King
21. My Resentment Disappeared 79
    By Chizobah Mary Alintah
22. The Pruning 83
    By Jessica Gallant
23. The Rare Gift 87
    By Kristin Faith Evans
24. Jonathan David 91
    By Howard Abrams
25. Zoe Karis 95
    By Hayden Walker, 1st Place Winner
26. A Woman Forsaken 99
    By Stephanie Rodda
27. From Devastation to Grace 103
    By Patricia Simmons Taylor
28. Trusting God Through It All 107
    By Tracy Riggs
29. The Long Road Back to Me 111
    By Susan Deitz Shumway
30. Despair to Repair 115
    By Cheryl Gore Pollard
31. The River of Life 119
    By Richelle Hatton
32. Living with a One-Armed Man 123
    By Terrie Todd, 3rd Place Winner
33. Loving an Addict 127
    By Stephanie Logan
34. Goodbye Mountain 133
    By Frances King Abrams
35. Will Someone Please Tell Me When to Breathe? 137
    By Kathy Stephens
36. Looking Through the Ether of Things 141
    By Ann-Elizabeth Blair Watt
37. Not. That. Story 145
    By Gayle Childress Greene
38. Extra Blessings 149
    By Karla Dee

39. My Breast Cancer Journey   153
    By Jeanette Botha
40. Facing Cancer with Faith   157
    By Karen O. Allen
41. Drifting with Jesus   161
    By Mary ScullyD
42. Breaking Through the Labyrinth of Mental Illness   165
    By Sharon Atwood
43. Don't Ask Why, Ask What   169
    Esther M. Bandy
44. Surrender   173
    By Christel Owoo
45. Undiagnosed   177
    By Jeanette Green
46. Aftermath of Showing Up   181
    By Joe S. Kimbrough II
47. Offering Hope to People Who Need God   185
    By Jim Jones with Richard Greene, 2nd Place Winner
48. I Was Blind but Now I See   189
    By Rebecca S. Carlisle
49. The Sword   193
    By Larry Mance

Questions for Personal Reflection/Group Study   197
About the Author   239

INTRODUCTION

Hayden Walker's world turned upside down when doctors discovered her unborn daughter had an extremely rare skeletal disorder. She endured "moments of utter brokenness" during the next few months awaiting delivery as "impending death wiggled in [her] womb." Her daughter, Zoe, died shortly after delivery, and, in deep sorrow, Hayden "chose the wood for Zoe's casket instead of her crib."

Vietnam veteran Jim Jones, a nurse anesthetist, and his wife, Linda, vacationed at Disney World until a horrific headache and severe gastric pain sent Jim to the hospital. Doctors told him he had suffered a minor stroke, one that erased his career-related memory and caused him to "hang up [his] scrubs."

Two days before their eighteenth wedding anniversary, Terrie's husband, Jon, caught his right arm in heavy machinery at work, mangling his arm and requiring an amputation five inches above his elbow. The physical mutilation brought tears, anger, and frustration to their family as they struggled with the painful loss.

Hayden, Jim, and Terrie suffered horrible, life-changing tragedies, difficult experiences that brought pain, heartache,

INTRODUCTION

and loss to themselves and to their families. But each refused to allow the tragedy to crush them. Through their deep faith in God, and walking slowly step-by-step with Christ through the painful fog, each turned devastating tragedy into victorious triumph.

Within these pages, you'll read about others who suffered tragedies, people just like you and me who instead of wallowing in sorrow, turned to God, resting in and depending upon His transforming love and power, and rising triumphantly above their painful circumstances. And, just like Hayden, Jim, and Terrie, each takes a giant step beyond their own pain and healing, openly and honestly sharing their personal stories and, in doing so, becoming "wounded healers" to a world of fellow hurting humans.

In Scripture, Jesus warns believers that "in this world you will have trouble." Surely, few of us live lives unmarred by painful suffering—whether physical, emotional, mental, or spiritual. But Jesus also promises that "in Me you may have peace." As believers in Jesus Christ, the people sharing their intimate stories within this book have discovered firsthand Christ's hope: "But take heart! I have overcome the world." (John 16:33 NIV)

Our heartfelt prayer is that through these stories, written by Christians all over the world, you will be encouraged, given hope, and brought closer to Christ as you journey through your own personal tragedy and, with God's loving help, find triumph.

To help accomplish these goals, we have included a Bible study at the end of the book. Within this study, you'll be given Scriptural encouragement as you deal with your own life tragedies, as well as be guided to healing through your participation in the section "Questions for Personal Reflection/Group Discussion." This Bible Study has been designed to be used personally by individuals or by a discussion study group.

Each writer in this anthology is an active member of Christian Writers for Life, a private online community that inspires, teaches, helps, and encourages today's Christian writers to become published authors to readers worldwide.

For more information about Christian Writers for Life, please visit www.denisegeorge.org.

1

THE SHORE

BY DONNA KAY

Staying in a private beach house for a week in 1985 was just what two college girls needed. We got a great deal on the small house, and it didn't matter to us that it had no television.

One cloudy day, we were shocked to find we were the only people on the beach. "This is totally awesome! We have the whole beach to ourselves." We laid on our floats, talking and singing for hours.

"Good grief, this water is dark blue," I commented as I looked over the edge of my float. "What time is it?" I asked Annemarie, who was sporting her new waterproof Swatch.

"It's three o'clock," she answered as I sat up.

"Oh my goodness!" I screamed in fear as my eyes stared ahead. The buildings were barely visible. We had drifted out to sea.

"We are gonna die!" Annemarie wailed. Instinctively, we both flipped over to our stomachs, stuck our arms into the water, and paddled. We were met by stinging tentacles. Quickly, we removed our arms and looked down. Fear filled my heart as

I gazed at what looked like hundreds of jellyfish below us, every color and size imaginable. It was horrifying!

We had no choice but to paddle. A burning sensation met my arm with each stroke. Red welts formed on my skin. I tried not to think about the documentary I had seen about jellyfish. I knew somewhere in this vast ocean were some so poisonous they could kill us.

At one point, I raised my arm out of the water, exposing a huge jellyfish that had wrapped its tentacles around my arm. Screaming, I flung it. It flew through the air, landing on my back. I felt stings as I thrashed around, attempting to knock it off. In my frantic movement, I fell into the water and my float glided away.

Jellyfish began stinging my entire body. The only thing within reach was Annemarie, and I hastily climbed atop her back. With no other option, we paddled rapidly to my float, and I relocated.

Despite everything, I remained fairly calm until I saw the dark shadow under my float. As the shark passed beneath, my heart sank. *We are going to die out here.* I prayed Annemarie wouldn't see it, too, as it swam away.

I looked to my right and was alarmed. "Annemarie, don't panic," I said, pointing. The wide wall of thick rain moved toward us. "Hold onto my float and don't let go, no matter what."

The eerie wall came closer until it was upon us. The large drops were pelting and cold as they beat down. I held tightly to her float.

The downpour was so hard and ceaseless that I could not see if she was still there. When the rain passed, we paddled full force, even sliding down toward the bottom of our floats to kick as well.

"What time is it?" I panted.

"Six thirty," Annemarie sighed with exasperation. The waves were stronger, but the jellyfish were scarce as we neared the shore. While we struggled to get past the waves, a riptide attempted to pull us back out.

"I give up," Annemarie half-whispered. Her exhausted eyes blankly stared, and she lay her head on the float.

"You can't give up!" I pleaded, but she gave no response.

I had no choice. Sliding into the water, I grabbed the front corner of her float and swam, pulling her along. *She quit! I cannot believe she quit, but I cannot leave her.* The waves continuously slapped me in the face, but I focused on the shore. My arms and legs ached. *Keep swimming. Lord, please help me.*

My swimming pool popped into my mind. *I swam seventy laps every day this summer for absolutely no reason. In thirteen years, I have never swum laps. God has prepared me for this! He has made me a strong swimmer.* I swam with Annemarie in tow.

After four hours, we finally reached the shore. I called my mama, and she frantically informed me that Hurricane Elena was headed our way. During the night, we were forced to evacuate.

As I have grown older, I've realized that life is the ocean and God is the shore. You can be floating along in life, happy as can be, and suddenly things go bad. You are suddenly at a place you never thought you would be, and the jellyfish, sharks, and storms (sickness, family, or money problems ...) come along and try to destroy you.

Keep your eyes on God. No matter how many times you get slapped in the face by the waves of life, stay focused on Him. He will prepare you for what is to come.

* * *

Donna Kay has been a teacher for the past twenty years. She lives in Rome, Georgia. Donna has three grown children, writes as a hobby, and claims she is "living life with faith, family, and laughter."

2

SURGERY AT THIRTEEN YEARS OLD

BY LINDA WEAVER CLARKE

*L*ittle did I know that my life was about to change drastically! For the first time, I would be taking a different road ... an unfamiliar one that I had not gone down before.

In the summer of 1963, at the age of thirteen, the doctors found out I had scoliosis of the spine. The doctor put a body cast from my hips to just below my collarbone. Since I was now in a heavy cast, I wasn't able to climb a tree, race down the fields of our farm, ride a bike, or play softball. At an instant, my life had changed.

After four months, the doctor fused eleven vertebrae from my neck to my hips. Soon after my operation, I developed pneumonia, and they had to put a large plastic container around my bed to help me breathe. It was oxygen therapy.

After my operation, and for the next four months, I was unable to leave my bed. My parents put a hospital bed in the living room where I could watch TV, do schoolwork, and receive visitors.

This was a very difficult time for me because I was a tomboy at heart, and I didn't like being cooped up in the house. How I longed to go outside and run with the wind or lie down on our lawn in the backyard and eat a green apple! I wanted to swing from our willow tree and act out another adventure.

After a year in a body cast, the doctors replaced the cast with a stiff, plastic, tan-colored brace. They told me it looked like a Marilyn Monroe figure, but it really didn't resemble any figure at all. The doctors enjoyed teasing me. I had to wear that brace every day and night. It was much better than a body cast though because I was able to bathe. Yea!

Many months passed. With great joy, we finally went back to the hospital to take off my brace. I felt this was the happiest day of my life. I would be free again.

As Dr. Hess checked me, I could tell that something wasn't right. Holding my breath, I listened to him as he announced that I had a crack in my spine. Dr. Hess told me this was unusual, and I would have to have another operation.

My heart sank! I wanted to cry. I could not believe this was happening to me. Why couldn't I live a normal life of a teenager? Why did I have to go through these trials?

My parents and I went home with a heavy heart and agreed to pray for the next four months, asking the Lord to help me gain enough strength, both mentally and emotionally, to have another operation. Each time I prayed, unbeknownst to my parents, I asked God for a miracle. I did not want to have another operation and more casts.

"Why?" I asked my Father in Heaven one night. "Why do I have to go through these trials? I believe in miracles. Why can't I have a miracle?" With a broken heart and tears streaming down my cheeks, I begged, "Please, I want to be a normal teenager."

I grew spiritually at this time because I needed to lean on the Lord. I could not do this alone. I needed to know what faith was and how it worked. As I prayed, my strength and faith grew until I had enough strength emotionally. When the doctors announced I had to have the operation, I realized this was a trial I had to endure.

After my operation, I had to wear another cast. In the summer when it was hot, I would sprinkle baby powder down my back so I would smell sweet. It helped the many itches go away, which a cast seemed to provide. After my cast was taken off, I had to wear another body brace for twelve more months. All in all, I felt the Lord blessed me and helped the time fly quickly.

It was a beautiful summer day in 1966, and the sun was shining brightly as we arrived at the doctor's office to have my brace removed. Three years had passed, and I was sixteen years old. I had missed out on the normal life of a teenager.

During this time of trial, I learned that my trials were for my growth. Because of these trials, I was unusually close to our Heavenly Father, more so than the average teenager. I learned what faith was and how to pray more fervently. I knew that my Father in Heaven listened to my prayers and helped me through my trials.

* * *

Linda Weaver Clarke was raised in the Rocky Mountains of Southern Idaho and now lives in the red desert hills of southern Utah. She is the author of thirty-two books: historical romance, cozy mystery, swashbuckling romance, historical mystery romance, a children's book, and nonfiction. Linda works at the Family Search Center where she helps people find their ancestors so they can learn about their heritage. This story is an excerpt from her 2019 autobiography.

3

THE BATTLE BELONGS TO GOD

BY STEPHEN D. EDWARDS

The worst thing that ever happened to me took place in grade one. My teacher had me stand in front of the class to count to one hundred. I know that seems tame, but that's not all. When I messed up and said a number out of order, I had to sit down and try again the next day. The other students had to endure the same.

Still tame, right? I'm not done yet.

The other students jeered and taunted me, calling me stupid among other things. Yes. Right in front of the teacher.

She did nothing about it. This is where my memory gets a little cloudy, but she may have even encouraged them.

My reaction was silence. I concluded that she was mean, and I hated her. Regardless of whether she encouraged the others, my self-esteem took a nosedive.

For many days during that year, I didn't want to go back to class after lunch or recess and would stay out, returning whenever I wanted to. I don't recall any repercussions for that.

That's not the only hit to my self-esteem that I took, but it was the worst one.

I became a victim. As a young adult I found myself trying to escape the pain of my past with a non-chemical addiction that caused more pain and may have led me into depression if I wasn't already in the darkness.

About thirty-four years later, I dearly wanted to die. I had taken on a door-to-door commission sales job but was not able to do this job well. I made plans to commit suicide.

Three days later, I found myself trying to run an addiction recovery meeting, and nothing was going right. I prayed for the spirit of suicide to leave me. Right then, I had peace, and everything worked out that night.

I continued to pursue freedom from addiction. I began to develop an attitude of gratitude, adopt a lifestyle of forgiveness, and read the bible daily, more than ten chapters per day. And I began to heal.

Gratitude came in little steps such as becoming thankful for the usual things like clothes to wear, food to eat, and a roof over my head. I grew to be more grateful by posting a small gratitude list to social media every day. That list was just three things for which I was grateful that were different from the previous day's posts. I didn't know I had twenty-one items to be grateful for!

Today, there is nothing that escapes my gratitude list. I'm grateful for everything in my life, even having suffered from depression.

I also tackled forgiveness. In order to heal, I had to let go of resentments. I found out that resentment was like a dose of poison I would continue to take for each resentment. Even in small doses, it was only going to harm me. The other person was not going to die. Not now. Not ever. Having said that, it wasn't so easily done. I said to myself in my mind that I forgive everyone, but in my heart, I held back on forgiving some offenses.

Then God revealed to me that those things were still unresolved. When I forgave, He healed that part of my life. I forgive easily now, before the offense has a chance to become a resentment.

The next big thing I had to fix was trust. I had a conversation with my mentor who told me that I needed to trust God, and that when I did, I would be able to trust others as well, and everything would fall into place. I did that. He is right. Along with that, God increased my faith and gave me great hope. He also told me that even though He healed the depression, life struggles would continue.

Depression finally gave way to joy, leaving me healed. I haven't looked back. I learned that life is better when I don't try to be perfect or expect people to be perfect. I no longer compare myself to others or my circumstances to their circumstances either. I found that gratitude and forgiveness are the pillars of joy.

Lastly, I stay grounded in the Word of God by reading the Bible every day because the moment I realized that depression had gotten the kick-to-the-curb, I was reading Scripture.

Going forward, I leave most of my life to God, because the battle belongs to Him.

* * *

Stephen D. Edwards began writing in his teen years but lost the passion for it. After gaining freedom from depression, he wrote a memoir titled *The Branch and the Vine* to share his experience to help those who suffer. The memoir is available at Kobo and Amazon. With his passion reignited, he now writes Christian themed short stories and novels to encourage and inspire. Edwards's most recent work has been published in *Agape Review*.

4

THE "L" ON MY FOREHEAD

BY NANCY LEE BETHEA

I felt the weight of my first-grade report card as I carried it home in my red and blue book satchel. The folded piece of white cardstock represented communication between two authorities in my life: my schoolteacher and my parents. Delivery of said document was my job, not its interpretation.

"Let's see, Nancy," my mom said as she perused my first-ever official school report card. "Looks like you're doing well in all your subjects." She then turned over the card and read the comments section on the back.

"What does it say?" I asked, hoping for her explanation. My six-year-old self had read the comments earlier but had been unable to process them.

"It says, 'Nancy needs to practice more self-control, especially when it comes to talking in class,'" my mom read aloud.

"What does that mean?" I did not know if my teacher thought I talked too much or too little.

"It means you're too chatty in class," she said with a smile.

"Just use the two ears God gave you and listen more than you talk."

With that advice, she hopped up and started preparing supper for our family of eight.

The next day during our morning devotion time, my dad prayed for each of his six children by name. When he got to me —the youngest—he said, "And please help Nancy learn to talk less and listen more at school." My five older siblings chuckled at this but remained silent.

I do not remember a drastic change in my loquaciousness, but by the time I reached fifth grade, my teachers commented on what a good student *and listener* I was. Their descriptions of me often included the words "quiet" and "thoughtful."

God developed my listening abilities to the point I could easily repeat verbatim something I heard only once. This came in handy during high school when I studied little for tests and did well because I listened in class. My friends told me their innermost secrets (even though I did not ask for them), and my teachers viewed me as a good kid, probably because I remained quiet (at school, at least).

Through the years, I have learned listening—truly paying attention and focusing on what someone is saying—is a gift we can offer others. As the noise in our society increases, the act of listening becomes more and more prized.

The adage says talk is cheap. Perhaps it is getting even cheaper in our modern day. But listening is priceless. Truly hearing someone shows how much we value them and what they have to say. We cheat ourselves and others when we divide our focus between people and our ever-present technological devices.

When people want to talk to me, which is often, I pocket my phone or close my laptop and focus on what they are saying. Sometimes, I think there must be a big "L" on my forehead for "Listener" because people talk to me everywhere I go!

Being a good listener is an affirming way to illustrate how God is always available to hear us. Psalm 18:6 says, "In my distress I called to the Lord; I cried to my God for help. From his temple, he heard my voice; my cry came before him, into his ears."

When we pray, He patiently listens to our heart's hopes and woes, dreams and hurts, pleas, and questions.

I encourage you to listen to the people around you. In doing so, you will show them honor and respect. You will also display, on a human level, a picture of how God listens to us when we pray.

But be prepared. People may start seeing an "L" on your forehead too!

* * *

Nancy Lee Bethea teaches Creative Writing at LaVilla School of the Arts in Jacksonville, Florida. She is also a freelance writer. She's currently working on a young adult novel and wondering where to put the boxes and boxes of journals she's kept for more than fifteen years.

5

CONNECTING IN DIFFICULT TIMES

BY RUTH "RENO" ANDERSON

She ranted and she raved. According to her, I was not worthy of her time. I was different than her, and that was enough to create a huge gap between us, she said. Yet we were both sisters in Jesus, we both had the same Holy Spirit living in each of us, and we both knew that we needed to be living in peace with each other. So why was she so scared of a discussion with me?

I have been talking and listening to other Christians in the USA and Canada and have become increasingly concerned about the lack of connection between Christians who are different from one another. Especially people like the woman I just mentioned. She said she was a believer and yet had no tolerance for someone who had a different skin color than she did. In light of current events that included the incendiary death of George Floyd, the riots, the heated arguments, and even the politicizing of our faith, I decided to talk to a friend.

That friend, Alexis, is different than me. She just turned thirty, and I am well over sixty. She has five children under ten, and I have seven grandchildren, the youngest who is fifteen. She lives in the heat of the southern USA, and I live in the freezing cold of western Canada. Oh, yeah, she is black, and I am white. I have lived in Africa, and Alexis has never left the USA. So how were we friends?

Alexis and I met in a Facebook group and quickly realized we had more in common than we had differences. We both loved teaching the Bible to others, and we both loved to find ways to encourage others toward a closer connection to God. We both loved music and reading too. We decided to join our two Bible study groups (hers: Daughters of the King; mine: Fierce Everyday Warriors) for a number of Zoom Bible studies (seven in all), being open and honest about our lives, and sharing our mutual struggles and triumphs as we journeyed in faith.

While there were some hiccups, our two groups celebrated our differences and our similarities. We made new friends, and we discovered some new ways of looking at life, at faith, and at family relationships. We studied worship music and the biblical truths behind our chosen songs (contributed by both groups on either side of the border) and were delighted to learn new music and hear stories. We learned that Galatians 2 tells us that racism is sin and has no place in the believer's heart or mind. We learned we could bridge the gaps between us and people who were different than us. That the Holy Spirit who was in all of us united us and could not divide us if we listened to God's Word and to the leading of the Holy Spirit to love all believers.

We learned to look at people one person at a time, not as a group about whom we had pre-conceived ideas. The labels we were putting on other believers because they are different than us, is not based on principles we see in God's Word. If we can see each person as an individual, find out the things we have in common with that person, look that person in the eye, and then pray for that fellow believer, it would make all the difference in the world.

Is there a cost to bridging that gap that seems to divide us from other believers when they are different than us? Of course there is. We had to get out of our comfort zone, we had to risk being rebuffed, and we had to open up our inner selves to other believers.

If connecting with other believers who are different than you is scary, start by saying "Hello." Have an open mind. Be interested in the other person. Take the first step. Assume you have things in common as Jesus-followers. Pray for opportunities to make new friends and embrace the uncomfortable.

I urge you to take responsibility for your thoughts and actions and intentions to our fellow believers and all human beings. I want to be accountable to my fellow Christians and to God for how I treat others. With me, would you resolve to not tolerate any level of prejudice, and to be totally open to anyone God sends our way? Think of someone who is different than you and say, "I will honor you as a fellow Jesus-follower." And then just love them, as Jesus wants us to do.

* * *

Reno Anderson lives in the prairies of western Canada now but has lived in three countries and traveled to over forty. She loves to travel, write, read, and learn new things. Her husband is the Lead Pastor of a small-town church, and she teaches Bible studies and does promotional work for the church. A published author of six books, she is a retired chaplain and educator. She is retired from work but still working on being a fierce everyday warrior for Jesus. Ruth "Reno" Anderson is co-author of the book *She is Not Different: Bridging the Gaps with Jesus When People are Different Than You* (co-authored with Alexis K. Brown).

6

MUCH LIKE JOSEPH

BY DESIRE NANA

Finding a job in Cameroon was like trying to put a camel through a needle eye. I got hired in Douala as electrician supervisor. I was placed number two behind the French ex-pat named Bertrand to supervise all electric works in the base, and other electricians as well. After years of praying and fasting, the Lord was gracious enough to open a door for me to find a job in a construction company located in Douala. But the road construction project was in Bertoua in the east part of Cameroon.

I went to Bertoua to manage the electric department with Mr. Bertrand, who was already working in the job site to help build some living spaces for French ex-pats. I met with Bertrand and other electricians on the base hired by Bertrand.

Just Like Joseph's brothers in the Bible, Bertrand and one of the electricians named Judah did not like the fact I was the youngest and most educated electrician in the team. Both became jealous of me, especially Judah who was a Cameroonian like me who believed that I took his place as number two in the team. Judah never accepted my leadership because he had the support of Bertrand with whom he was a friend.

But through God's grace, I did my job very well and resolved every single challenge that we had. I was known to be the smartest electrician. But Judah and Bertrand didn't like that, and they became even more jealous. Their jealousy grew to hatred like Joseph and his brothers, and they formulated their plan to get me fired. But in the midst of all that, I continued to show God's love to them.

Judah and Bertrand were successful in getting me fired because the director of the entire project did not know what was going on in the field. After I was fired, I packed all my belongings and went back to Douala. But God was working amid this chaos. The Lord was using those two like he used Joseph's brothers to accomplish His purpose in my life.

Being fired, or being thrown in an empty cistern, or being sold to slavery was not good for either of us. I had put all my hope on that job to make money, and to leave the country in search of a better life. But that hope got crushed. I started to worry about the whole situation. But instead of letting worry drag me down, I resolved to trust the Lord.

The next day after I arrived in Douala, I met a brother named Nya, and as we were chatted, he mentioned a lottery program that people played to go to the United States. He also mentioned the name of a brother who could help me play. I met the brother and he helped me fill out a form. I attached a four-by-four picture and mailed the envelope to the US.

A few weeks after being fired, I got a call from the director of the project in Bertoua stating that nothing was working on the jobsite since I had left. He wanted me back as soon as possible. He presented his excuse to me for not knowing I was the brain of the electrical department I had accepted. But I conditioned my return to the jobsite, and he accepted all my conditions. I was on the job site the next day to fix everything that was not working. Bertrand and Judah were fired before I even got on the jobsite. I would, later on, learn that Judah was hospitalized. I paid him a visit and prayed with him.

I fixed everything in two weeks, and I spent the rest of the time doing maintenance. After four months back on the job, I got a phone call from my uncle in Douala. I had used his address as the return address on my visa application. He said I had a letter coming from the US. I was surprised because I had completely forgotten about playing the lottery.

I told my boss about the situation, and he was kind enough to let me go to Douala to see my uncle. As soon as I got in his office, he presented me with the letter. When I opened the envelope, I read the word "congratulations" in the header of the letter, congratulating me for winning the DV-Lottery.

Bertrand and Judah meant evil against me by getting me fired, just like Joseph's brothers meant evil against him when they threw him in the cistern and sold him to slavery. But God meant good, because all these evildoings were part of His plan.

Nothing is too big or too difficult for our Lord, so I learned not to worry about anything anymore, but to let God know my problem because He is always working behind the scenes to make our dreams come true.

* * *

Desire Nana was born in Cameroon, Central Africa, where he grew up. By God's grace and miracle, he was able to immigrate to the U.S. in 2002, and he joined the U.S. Navy that same year. Even though English was not his first language, he managed to learn English in the military, giving him the confidence he needed to pursue his undergrad and graduate school education. He is the father of four girls.

7

GOD KNOWS

BY WOLFGANG BERNHARDT

*A*fter successfully finishing my school years, I was faced with a choice: Do I join a chemical company as a learner technician, or do I go to university to study medicine? On the advice of my mother, who offered to pay for my university studies, I chose the latter.

I passed my first two years at medical school, but near the end of my second year I started having doubts about medicine as a career. I reasoned that many people have to consult doctors because of their unhealthy lifestyle. My dilemma was that I could not see myself having the courage to tell my (future) patients that if they changed their lifestyle, they would not need to see a doctor.

The mental turmoil brought about by this dilemma became so strong that shortly before my third-year exams, I walked out of university and hitch-hiked home.

My parents thought I had gone out of my mind! They refused to accept my reasoning. They accused me of being ungrateful for the sacrifice they were making to pay for my studies and said that I was irresponsible and reckless. I was accused of being spineless, not having the guts to finish what I had started. Early the following year, they insisted I go back to university and ask the authorities to allow me to continue my studies.

The dean of the medical faculty listened to my story, but he said that before he would re-admit me, I was to see a psychiatrist. He arranged for the head of the psychiatric department of the hospital to examine me. His diagnosis was schizophrenia. I was admitted to the psychiatric ward and put on strong tranquillizer medication, as well as a course of electro-convulsive therapy (ECT).

During my eight-week stay in hospital, I had time to reflect on my decision. During these dark days, the regular visits by my sister, a nursing sister in the same hospital, buoyed my spirit. I also received a visit from the pastor of the Lutheran church I had been attending and in whose choir I sang. When he visited me, all he did was pray for me, then he left a little card that had a Scripture verse from Psalms promising a blessing to those who dig wells in the valley of desolation. This message hit home and spoke to me. During that time, I was also convicted to put right a thoughtless and selfish deed I had done to a friend many years earlier. As soon as I had done that, I again saw hope for the future, and I started to get better. I decided that to give up medicine was the right decision.

After my discharge from hospital, I went back home. My dad, who was one of the senior managers in a textile factory, gave me a job as an assistant fitter. The long hours of assembling rows and rows of machines gave me time to reflect on my decision and start making plans for the future.

The next year, I registered in the engineering faculty of our local university in the discipline of chemical engineering. I had to start from first year again because the subjects were different from those studied in medicine. Despite the fact I had to continue taking tranquillizer medicines, which severely affected my concentration and alertness levels, I eventually managed to get my degree.

Gradually, my parents changed their mind about me. After all, I was not a quitter. We learned to accept each other, and our relationship was restored.

Sometimes people close to us make decisions we cannot understand. We think those decisions are wrong, and in our love and concern for them we want them to "do the right thing." We put inordinate pressure on them to "see sense." This can cause deep hurt and leave long-term scars. It is important to accept with grace the decisions other people make, and give them the freedom to choose, even when we think they are making a massive mistake.

* * *

Dr. Wolfgang Bernhardt is a professional engineer. He holds a PhD in Chemical Engineering from the University of KwaZulu Natal. He is a member of the accreditation committee for the Engineering Council of South Africa. He and his wife have four adult children—a teacher, two medical doctors, and a pastor.

8

MUSIC—MY CALLING!

BY LYNNE DRYSDALE PATTERSON

*D*id you know what you wanted to be when you grew up? From the time I was a young girl growing up in St. Petersburg, Florida, I believed music was my calling. Music is in my family bloodline. In fact, you might say, I was "born into" a musical family. I really had no say-so.

My great-grandparents were traveling minstrels. My grandfather headed the Philadelphia office of ASCAP (American Society of Composers, Authors and Publishers) before retiring to St. Petersburg. My grandmother taught high school English and, later, Sunday school in a still largely attended church in St. Pete. My mother played piano and our home was filled with music.

Sitting in our Florida room, ear pressed to the stereo, I listened to a variety of popular music. What was the mood? What about those words and rhythms? I memorized songs while singing into a beautiful gold gilt dining room mirror from my great-grandparent's dining room, my mother's childhood home in Wynnewood, Pennsylvania, our family home in St. Pete, and which adorns my dining room today. While gazing into that mirror, I decided I wanted to become a singer, songwriter, recording artist.

Life was fun growing up in St. Pete. We were members of The St. Petersburg Yacht Club, where I sang in the Grille Room for the first time. As members of one of the local country clubs, we were on the golf course Saturdays and Sundays. Each year my sister and I were given new Easter dresses, and our family attended my grandmother's church.

But I had a sneaking suspicion life was not as it seemed. On the inside, I began feeling lost and disconnected. In hindsight, I realize no one in my family could answer the deepest longing of my soul. They didn't know what to say.

Because of my love of music and natural affinity for singing, I began writing songs, journaling, and writing poetry in junior high. My sister dabbled with the guitar, and I began playing the guitar—by ear. I sat in my bedroom for hours learning songs and writing my own.

Eventually, through booking agents who were members of our country club, I was booked to sing and play my guitar at resorts and college concert venues. Yet, as I learned to interact with audiences across the country, I was still that little kid inside wondering what is really going on. I placated my anxiety with, "I'm on my way." But my question became, " ... on my way to what?"

Yet, I thought, surely if I can just get *"there,"* everything will be alright. I began my quest reading works of contemporary philosophers. At the encouragement of reputable music business friends, I moved to Nashville. After signing a contract with a song publisher, and garnering interest from a record label, I realized that accomplishing my goal could not bring that deep inner satisfaction I desired. What I thought would fill my emptiness didn't, and when it didn't ... I remembered a lyric, *"Is That All There Is?"* But there's good news! That's *not* all there is!

The prominent couple from whom I rented a condo told me they were praying for the right tenant! I was that tenant! There was something about this couple; a certain peace I began to desire. As I shared philosophical gleanings with them, they spoke of Jesus Christ to me.

While sipping tea in their living room one afternoon, we began discussing the Bible. I knew about the Bible. But my childhood Sunday school teachings were nothing more to me than cute stories. No one told me the Bible is God's special way of revealing His Love for us; that the Bible is God's "Owner's Manual," with instructions on how He designs our lives to work. Adam and Eve, the original parents, sinned in the Garden of Eden when they disobeyed God. Everyone is born into Adam and Eve's family. We really have no say-so! Just as having no say-so as to being "born into" the musical genes of my family bloodline, I had no say-so in being born into the sin nature bloodline of Adam and Eve. And because I was born with a sin nature, how could I, a sinner, stand before Holy God? I could not! That lost, disconnected feeling from childhood was my longing to know God, to be connected to Him, and to have a personal relationship with Him. God, Himself, was calling me!

That afternoon, I prayed with Ben and his wife, and I invited Jesus Christ to come into my life and forgive my sins! No longer do I look into an ancestral antique gold gilt mirror for identity. I open the Bible and see my reflection in the mirror of God's Word. And the rest, as they say, is HIS-story!

* * *

Lynne Drysdale Patterson, an award-winning Christian singer/songwriter, author, with songs on Dove and Grammy Award-winning records, wrote *Taproots of Tennessee: Historic Sites and Timeless Recipes* published by the University of

Tennessee Press. Her middle grade stories are published by *Clubhouse Magazine*. Lynne and her engineer, classically trained guitarist husband, Bruce, live in Nashville.

9

THE SHIPWRECK

BY TERESA NEWTON-TERRES

*E*very family has secrets.
    Not everyone's include a shipwreck.

I know what it's like to feel caught in a torrent of emotions, not understanding why an event happened.

You see, my father was lost at sea when I was two years old. I overheard talk of a shipwreck, submarine, secret science test, and kidnapping. Yet no one talked to me. I grew up, but still, no one talked about the shipwreck. This created in me unresolved questions, misplaced anger, and unanchored trust.

Later, I lost my mother when my soldier-husband and I lived on an island. Then, we moved from our seaside to a land-locked home.

My soldier encouraged me to join a Grief Share group. Among this fellowship, I experienced a normal journey of *grief*, until the session on childhood loss surfaced.

I joined a different fellowship and attended a leadership class. We reviewed *feelings* experienced due to change. Apparently, the feelings about change are those of grief—denial, anger, depression, letting go, testing, search-for-meaning, and internalization—which can shipwreck results or, like a spaceship, catapult results into new frontiers.

Leaders were expected to take ownership of those under their stewardship. Thus, I took ownership of my feelings.

My mind navigated back to a time before my mother's loss. A secret scrapbook arrived. My grandmother had compiled it and then hid it. After a relative found it, they sent it. As my mother and I reviewed the shipwreck, I gained new perspectives.

"Once, you asked me if I was angry at God," I said.

"You said, 'No,'" she said.

"I was grateful that you didn't ask me, 'Who are you *angry* with?'"

"Why?"

"I remember the day of the shipwreck. I was dragged around by one arm. Then you put me in a car and escaped to a safe harbor. I was begging you to tell me what happened. I wrote a letter to Grandmother asking what happened. No one understood me. No one responded. I was angry at *you* because *you* didn't rescue daddy!"

How crazy is that?

Then the wave of memory carried me to a time when I was a young mother dragging my daughter by one arm. I put her into a car and escaped to a safe harbor. Later, I returned. The abuse continued. I was alive but divorced, depressed, and desired revenge after a four-year marriage. I submerged my shame and blamed my decisions.

On a walk, a relative asked, "What do you think your father would be like?"

Bewildered, I stopped.

"Our Father, who art in heaven …" I pray. Yet I never considered the difference between my father, a mere man, and my God.

Who do I worship?

The wave of memory encircled another childhood perception: "Daddy's decision to get on that ship, the *Marie*, was a bad one." Curious, I wondered who am I to judge that decision. Perhaps judgment belongs to God?

Later, in another fellowship, we considered biblical forgiveness as living waters. It began in a personal relationship with God.

Embracing the child within me, I prayed, "My heavenly Father, God, I've judged the worthy, honored the unworthy, shamed the beloved because my anchor wasn't secured with a trust in you. I'm so sorry. Please forgive me?" And in timeless truth I read, "You are forgiven."

With my soldier's leadership, we asked God to take ownership of our lives and be the leader of our home. Like a spaceship we launched into new frontiers of companionship as my soul mate and I walked side by side toward eternity.

How crazy is that?

There are things you don't want to get good at. Like, *good grief*.

After his thirty-five years of military service, twenty-four years of marriage, and six years of retirement, I lost my husband to a massive heart attack.

I returned to a visual, charting the feelings of grief. I embraced it.

"I TRUST YOU," I worshipped.

Like many families, my family is complicated. As the matriarch of a blended family, I took ownership for stewardship of the journey of grief my family would travel. And, like a spaceship, we launched into new territories. That was seven years ago.

Finding answers to my father's disappearance was the only item on my bucket list, which launched a quest. Along the way, it led to treasures—friendships, a documentary, a museum exhibit, a commemoration, healing hearts, and a memoir about a shipwreck, *Mystery of the Marie*!

I know how to navigate the stormy seas of life to experience not one shipwreck but seven ships—leadership, fellowship, ownership, companionship, stewardship, spaceship, and worship.

Life is a treasure hunt, so keep tracking, keep trusting, and keep treasure hunting. And for all the questions that are unanswered, and the secrets that are submerged, I found a place of rest as I trust in God.

* * *

Teresa Newton-Terres, an award winning Project Management Professional (PMP), authored a hot aerospace cold case untold story, *Mystery of the Marie*, her childhood tragedy that surfaced a Cold War secret (with co-author James Pence). Teresa finds passion and peace in sunrises and sunsets by seas, in mountains, around the world.

10

TO ERR IS HUMAN

BY LINDA MARIE

My dad committed suicide when I was eighteen years old. He was the parent I was closest to, the parent I thought I could always count on. I was shocked and afraid, although I had seen both of my parents suffer with severe depression.

Their beginning together had been so promising. They were both intelligent and kind people, she a nurse and he a pilot in the Navy. But they both entered marriage with many problems from their childhoods, addictions, and medical problems that would surface later. They divorced when I was seven years old and then remarried each other when I was twelve. We moved every year. There was constant yelling and inconsistency in our home.

As I grew up, my mother had a tremendous amount of anger, and she took it out on me. I, in turn, began to have a lot of my own anger. My father, in an effort to compensate for the lack of care on my mother's part, and to protect me from her abuse, did not discipline me. Human love is not perfect. In later years it was difficult when I had to learn what it is to be disciplined. But I am so thankful my dad loved me unconditionally. Because I had this experience with an earthly father, I am able to identify with God as a loving Father. However, at the time of my dad's death, I was devastated and felt abandoned by both my earthly and heavenly Father.

The night of my father's death, he made my boyfriend leave earlier than usual, and he told me to go to bed. I would ordinarily sit up and talk to him, but this night he was adamant. I didn't understand. I even said, "Why are you doing this? You're never like this" And he said again, "Go to your room and go to sleep." I went up the stairs to my room, saying, "I hate you."

That was the last thing I said to my father. When I found out he had killed himself, I realized why he had wanted me to go to bed. I was filled with such remorse that I had been angry at him, that I would never get to say I was sorry. I worried that his death was my fault. I didn't have much time to think about these things because only weeks after my dad died, my mother threw me out of the house. I was in college and had to drop out. I had no job and nowhere to go, but God looked out for me. One of our neighbors took me in.

In the years that followed, I was successful in business, had built my own house, and then married the wrong person. He began to use drugs and he cheated on me. During a torrential rainstorm, the house was hit by lightning. The roof was burned off and it flooded from the roof down. I was then twenty-seven years old and had stayed away from church since my father's death, But the next day, I saw a cross on the steeple of a church, and I felt drawn to go in and say a prayer. By coincidence, or God-incidence, I had wandered into a church that had also been hit by lightning on the same day as my house.

Then the real work of my life began. I started to go to church again and read my Bible. I got on my knees and poured my heart out to God. All the years of sorrow and disappointment came out in a flood of tears. I had been through so much. I began to take an honest look at my marriage. I realized that I had a part in its failure. I had brought my childhood anger into that relationship. God began to teach me about mercy and forgiveness. As I learned to forgive myself, and was kinder to myself, I felt less anger towards others. I worked for years on forgiveness of my mother. She died when I was fifty years old, and she was much the same as she had been in my teenage years. But I had changed. As I learned more about my mother's life, I began to feel true compassion for her and to pray for her.

Some healings don't come in this lifetime. My parents' greatest consistency, and greatest gift, to me is that even with all their problems, they were open with their love of God. My dad made sure we went to church, and my mom would continually speak of Jesus and of how He understood her. As a Christian, I have the confident hope that one day I will see them again in heaven, healthy and whole.

* * *

Linda Marie is a Stephen Minister, has a Certificate of Spiritual Direction and Theology, and was inducted into the Honor Society for Religion and Theology. She is author of a devotional, *Forty Footsteps*, and of children's books (*Cleo Goes to Rio, Cleo Goes Ballooning, Cleo's Family Tree*). Her books are available on Amazon.

11

GOD'S PROMISES

BY CAROLYN KAZMIERCZAK

I've always heard it said that losing a child is the most devastating kind pain you will ever endure, and I believe that to be true, because I have children and grandchildren. But when my father unexpectedly and tragically passed away at age eighty-four, I experienced a kind of pain that absolutely consumed me.

I questioned God with that all too familiar question: "Why?" I was scared. What if my father didn't know Jesus? He had told me many years earlier that he had accepted Christ as a young adult. But over the years, I had grown to believe my father had never really embraced his new life in Christ, and that frightened me.

Scripture in Acts 16:31 speaks about a Philippian jailer who placed his faith in Jesus. *"Believe on the Lord Jesus Christ, and you will be saved, you and your household."* After my father's death, this Scripture overwhelmed my thoughts night after night through heavy tears as I pleaded with God to promise me that He had saved my father. I wanted to believe that because I was saved, the Lord would make sure my household was saved too. This Scripture, of course, means that not only would the jailer become saved because of his faith in Christ, but his household would become saved because of their own personal faith in Christ. How this Scripture reads is not how it's meant, but I didn't care.

Years have passed by since my father's death, and I've had many tearful days of grieving and unrest concerning my father's salvation. But because of my faith in Christ, I've chosen to trust Him completely. I believe in His sovereignty, and I have finally come to believe that what my father had shared with me concerning his salvation is true.

My mother has since passed away, but her death was expected—not that that makes it any easier to endure. But it was my mother who first instilled a desire in me to know Christ. She took my sisters and me to church, taught us to tithe, and encouraged us in our faith. I have a peace that she is now celebrating with Jesus and is totally and completely healed of the dementia that so cruelly took her mind and her life.

Together my parents were the creators and originators of a campground and RV park—and not just *any* park. They built their park from nothing to something. It was just raw land purchased over fifty years ago, and it became a massive business. Everything they made and created was done by their own hands—backbreaking work to achieve a park with a swimming lake, cabins, reunion halls, bluegrass festivals, RV clubs, and church retreats. Their business was successful with no real tragedies or devastating destruction over a span of forty-five years. My parents lived a long life together, enjoying the fruits of their labor.

After my parent's deaths, my sisters and I sold their beloved park. Tragically, just shortly after the sale, two very large buildings burnt to the ground. One building was a museum, full of treasures and memorabilia. The other building was a favorite to many patrons who held their family reunions there year after year. The most recent tragedy was the dam breaking on the small swimming lake that my father had built. My father was a jack-of-all-trades, and he could make or build anything. My mother was a good wife, a good mother, and the hardest worker I'd ever known. I guess you could say without a doubt, I was and still am very proud of my parents.

I'm thankful my parents did not have to witness the tragedies that have come about to their little piece of heaven here on earth. If they had, I have no doubt they would have been absolutely devastated. They had reached an age that would have prevented them from being able to rebuild physically and emotionally.

I've cried a lot since the loss of my parents, and also over the tragic circumstances that have damaged their beautiful park. But I'm very thankful that my parents' legacy is being carried on by the new owners, as God has so generously met their needs for rebuilding.

I've learned to be thankful for God's promises and His assurances because I believe my parents are now living in the heavenly realms with Him for all eternity. And maybe they're even living in a more beautiful park than the park they had created here for themselves.

Being thankful for our parents is pleasing to God. And when their time here on earth is done, we can trust that our holy and sovereign God will give us the needed strength to live without them until that glorious day when we will see them again.

* * *

Carolyn Kazmierczak is a freelance writer for Christian magazines. She also teaches a ladies' Sunday School class filled with ladies she adores. She lives with her husband, Greg, in East Texas. They have two grown, married children and three grandsons: Jaxon, Luke, and Everett. Visit her website at www.reassuringhope.com.

12

TIME WAITS FOR NO ONE

BY ALBERTA SEQUEIRA

*I*n time, all of us will lose a parent, or both. As we age, it's supposed to be a natural acceptance in life ... until it hits us personally. My world came to an end (along with my mental state) when my father, Brigadier General Albert L. Gramm, came down with cancer. I wasn't prepared. He was eighty years old and claimed he still had too much left to do.

I never took the time to ask him about his life. He had been one of the commanding officers for the 26th Yankee Division and fought in WWII in Metz, the battle of Lorraine, and the famous Battle of the Bulge. Those years were buried deep within his soul to share only with his Army buddies.

I remember as a child, I would sit with my back against his armchair with my arms wrapped around both his legs as he smoked his pipe watching *Victory at Sea*, one of his favorite shows. Very little was said between us, but there was shared time for love.

The final pain came when we called hospice in Yarmouth Port, Massachusetts, to help us say goodbye to him. Our brother Joe and his wife, Marge, bought a house in South Dennis,

Massachusetts, to care for him and my mother in his last days. He never got to enjoy his new surroundings for long.

Finally, he could no longer get up. His time was spent on morphine, going in and out of consciousness. My twin brother, Albert, my sister, Leona, and two younger brothers, Bill and Joe, crammed our last days with him. My mother walked in a numb state, acting as if nothing was happening. Hospice warned us that was a sign of her not wanting to accept him leaving her. In fact, they said, some get angry at the one dying.

When my father had been in the war on foreign land, he had promised Our Blessed Mother that if she got him home safely to his family, he would say the rosary every day until he died.

We were brought up as strong Catholics who attended Mass every Sunday. If we missed going with our father, we had better go to another service.

My sister, Leona, and my sister-in-law, Marge, ran around the house to collect the extra rosaries. Leona asked Dad if he wanted us to say the prayer for him and he could follow. I was embarrassed to admit in my forties I had no idea how to say them. When we received our first Holy Communion, each child was given a rosary. I honestly think that most of them went into a drawer, never to be seen again. I was one of those children never to learn them.

I followed the family with the rosary for the first time. I realized the holy prayer was the story of Jesus and Mary's life in the five decades. I had left the Church for years, and as I watched my father with his deep devotion and love for Our Lady, I realized that I not only needed God back in my life, but I wanted Him.

My thoughts went back to my reasons for leaving the Church. I had stopped practicing my faith. I had lived fourteen years with an alcoholic husband, and I became an enabler, only to bring him deeper into his addiction. He died at forty-five years of age at the VA Hospital in Providence, Rhode Island. I felt God had abandoned me, so I stopped going to Mass and saying prayers.

After our father died, I took his rosary and prayer book home and have found my way back to God. I took a ten-day pilgrimage to Medjugorje in Bosnia to witness four out of six visionaries having apparitions with Our Blessed Mother. It's there that I had witnessed miracles, not only with myself, but with my husband, Al, who returned to Church.

My daughter, Lori, died in 2006, at thirty-nine years of age, from alcohol and drug abuse, as did her father. I believe turning back to God and my faith came from my father—my gift from him. Doing so helped me cope with my loss. I turned my pain and sorrow into helping others. I'm an author who wrote about my husband and daughter and became a professional speaker on alcohol and drug abuse in private and public events.

Miracles do happen. God never closes the door on us. We are the ones who have to open our hearts to let Him into our soul. If we open our eyes and become alert, there may be a person who enters our life to lead us back to our faith. There isn't a day that I don't start and end with prayer, no matter how good or bad the day became.

* * *

Alberta Sequeira is the author of several books on alcohol and drug abuse, having lost her husband and grown daughter to their battles with substance abuse. She hopes her experiences can be a help to others. Alberta lives in Massachusetts, and her books are available on Amazon.

13

JANETTA, YOU WILL ALWAYS MATTER

BY JANETTA FUDGE MESSMER

*G*rowing old erased Dad's ability to dream. At ninety-one, his body didn't let him do the things he'd done a few years before. His eyes that had sparkled when he ventured to his shed to tinker on a project now dimmed with despair. His still sharp mind couldn't grasp how his body finally failed him.

But the final straw came when Mom and I wheeled him into the nursing home, the place he said he never wanted to go. As we settled him in, he stated that his life didn't matter anymore, and he wanted to die. "What good am I anyway?"

My father's words broke my heart. I had to fight back tears before I answered: "Dad, you do matter. More than you'll ever know." And he did matter to me and his family. But the look on his weathered face only spoke defeat.

Oh, Dad, I wish I could wave a magic wand and make you a vibrant man once again. How I long to turn the clock back so I could again watch you, the person who dreamed the impossible and made it happen on occasion. I'd love to see the sparkle return to your eyes when an idea for an invention popped into your head.

But I can't turn back the clock. Time and the ravages of age have crept in and stolen you away from us. For this, I'm so very sad. But there is something I can do. I can honor your legacy with my own life.

From now on, I'll spend more time dreaming. I'll tinker with something until it's how you would have done it. Dancing with my husband will become a priority because I know how much you and Mom enjoyed gliding across the floor.

I'll buy an extra lottery ticket—just for you, Dad. And, before the announcer reads the winning numbers, I'll ponder out loud, as you did, on how I'd spend the money. I know if you'd have ever won, you would have taken me along on a fun-filled adventure. And I'll write.

I hope you know how much I love you, Dad. Yes, age may have taken you away, but you're still alive in my soul. One day I will see you again. Then I will be able to tell you what you helped me do with the rest of my life.

I dreamed big dreams.

I wrote (and published) novels because you told me before you died to "keep going with your writing. I'm so proud of you."

And I thanked God that He gave me such a special man I got to call Dad. You are loved and missed.

***

Turning Life into Comedy is **Janetta Fudge Messmer**'s tagline. She loves to laugh, and it's why she writes Christian comedy (with a touch of romance). She's also published a Christian historical work and a thirty-day devotional. For Janetta, writing and traveling go hand in hand since she, her hubby (Ray), and their pooch (Maggie) are full-time RVers. Most days, you'll find them out sightseeing. But first, Janetta has to sit down and write a few words.

14

SAYING GOODBYE

BY PAM WADDELL

I was thirty-three years old when my mother died. Her death shook the very core of my faith. My mom came home from the Daytona Beach hospital under hospice care. I had no idea I would be fully responsible for her care. The hospice nurse set up all the equipment and gave me a crash course in administering injections and changing IV and colostomy bags.

Daddy didn't know how to deal with Mom's terminal cancer. So, he got up each morning, dressed, and went to work. It was the only way Dad knew how to cope. My heart screamed in protest, "This cannot be happening!" But it was happening, and Mom depended on me.

We settled into a daily routine. Mom's two closest friends became surrogate grandmothers to my children—taking them to the library, the beach, movies, and typical summer activities, shielding them from the dark side of cancer. Their evenings were spent in bed with their Nanny as she read them bedtime stories.

Days turned into weeks, and Mom slept more each day. I sat beside her on the bed, reading as she slept. I was there whenever she needed me. As I read one afternoon, Mom woke with the sweetest smile spreading across her face. She opened her eyes, smiling sleepily.

I asked, "Sweet dreams?"

She sighed, "I wish you could see. I just wish you could see …" and drifted off to sleep again. She didn't have to tell me. Her peaceful smile said it all. God was showing her where she was going. She beheld His glory. That was the last time my mother woke.

A few days later, as Dad got ready for work, Mom's breathing became very shallow, getting slower and slower. Daddy came over and sat down beside her as I felt her pulse slowly stop. My mother went to glory at the age of fifty-four, leaving us behind. My mind told me I would see her again, but my heart broke. I wanted to scream at God, to tell Him He had made a mistake. I was hurt and angry that God would take my mother.

Finally, my husband and extended family arrived. We leaned on each other to get through the funeral. When the funeral director asked if we were ready to close the casket, my dad and brothers nodded, mumbling, "Yes." But I couldn't move. I couldn't speak. I felt if I were to open my mouth, a hideous scream would escape. I couldn't swallow for the large lump lodged in my throat. My husband finally answered for me, and they lowered the top of her casket.

Once home, friends surrounded me with love and compassion. They had organized a prayer circle while I was away, and someone had prayed for me every hour of every day. Now I understood that God enabled me to care for my mother. I was never on my own.

A few weeks later, my pastor stopped me and asked how I was. I gave him my automatic answer, "I'm fine."

He smiled and hugged me and said, "Well, when you're ready to talk, I'll listen."

Another month went by before I began to lose control. I snapped at my children and argued with my husband over every little thing. He finally told me I needed to deal with my "issues" and stop taking things out on him and the children. I was also short with customers at work. Reluctantly, I made an appointment with my pastor.

As I sat in Pastor A.L.'s office, he asked if I had cried. I realized I had not shed one tear. I feared if I ever started to cry, I wouldn't be able to stop. He knelt in front of me and encouraged me to let my feelings out. I sobbed, the knot in my throat escaping along with my cries of "Why my mom? Why not someone else's mother?"

At this, he looked at me and said, "Why would you say that?"

I sobbed, "Because I still need my mother!" At that, I let go. He held me as I cried until I had no more tears, his shirt wet from my tears. I left his office that day with my heart feeling whole for the first time in months.

It's been over thirty years since my mother died, and it still brings tears to my eyes, but I now understand Romans 8:28. I became a Christian counselor, training through the American Association of Christian Counselors. I volunteer as a grief counselor through my church and occasionally a local hospice organization to counsel children's grief groups. I use my loss and heartache to help others get through theirs. My story is a testament to God's power as felt through the prayers of others.

* * *

Pam Waddell is a published author of *Simply His*. She is a contributor in *Day by Day*, published by the Southern Christian Writers Conference. Pam has written scripts for children and youth programs and White Bible Ceremonies. She has been a Bible teacher in her home church for over thirty years.

15

I HEAR HIM

BY CHERYL SCHUERMANN

"*I* hear the Lord speaking to me."

"Really, Mom?" I whispered.

She nodded, "I hear Him. And He says I don't have much time."

Her words startled me. In the last stage of Alzheimer's disease, she had not spoken coherent words in many days. For several years, memories of family and friends and her beautiful life gradually faded. Toward the end, she spent most of her days trying to make sense of her surroundings. My heart broke for her so many times, I wondered if it would recover.

Day after day, I held her hands and rubbed lotion on her arms. I named all the members of her family and assured her of their love. I read Scripture to her. But this day she heard not just my voice, but the voice of the Lord. Did I hear Him, too? Did He have words for me? Had I even been listening?

After my father's sudden passing, we moved my mother to our community in a house just around the corner from us. Except on a rare occasion, Mom and I were together every day. Joined at the hip, one might say. As the disease progressed, we hired a part-time aide to help care for her. My husband disconnected some appliances in her home for her safety. I fished several cellphones out of the washing machine. For days, we searched high and low for her wedding rings that had vanished without a trace. She began calling me in the middle of the night, "Hey, Sister! Where are you? I'm ready for the day!" My clock often said 2:30 AM.

While managing my mother's fragile, declining health, my own autoimmune challenges increased. The responsibility of making every detailed decision for another adult's life took its toll both emotionally and physically. I often felt helpless, hopeless, and angry at the ugliness of the disease. The brain degeneration was progressive, and medical science offered nothing to stop it. Her symptoms only worsened. How could this happen to such a capable, resilient woman who had survived a childhood in northern Alaska? Even cancer several years earlier did not keep her down.

Looking back on those challenging years, I realize the Lord spoke to me, too. He taught me new ways to love and protect my mother. He taught me how to respond appropriately to her increasingly needy and often unusual behavior. He taught me how to enter her world and validate her thoughts and feelings.

When my mother shared about her deceased sister sitting on the end of the bed, I resisted the temptation to refute her story. Instead, I asked her to tell me about their visit. "Oh, and she wore a blue calico dress? I am sure it was lovely, Mom. I wish I could have seen her."

When she told me about the little men with machetes who climbed through the dining room windows, the Lord prompted me yet again. "What a funny sight! Well, they are gone now. They don't want to tangle with an Alaska pioneer!"

During the last six months of her life, she often thought it was her birthday. My natural inclination was to say, "Mom, your birthday is June 15, but when it comes around, we'll have a big party!" I used that line a few times before learning to say, "Wow! Happy Birthday! Let's celebrate!" A quick run for ice cream bars, a rousing Happy Birthday chorus, and we had a party. How many times did we celebrate her birthday during those months? A joyous dozen times or more.

How can someone triumph through the devastation of debilitating brain disease and dementia? How can caregivers learn to treasure each tender moment with those they love, no matter how fleeting? In Psalm 46:10, the Lord tells us to "be still, and know that I am God." He will win the battle, even in the midst of pain and suffering and heartbreak.

Allow God to fill you to overflowing with compassion and empathy for the suffering of those with dementia. Just as Jesus entered our world to minister to us, enter their world. Validate them as fully human, made in God's image. Help them preserve memories by telling family stories over and over again. Though our loved ones with dementia will lose much, we must never forget to embrace the power of grace. Those with dementia may lack awareness of self, but their spirit is intact, and they will one day stand before God completely restored in body and soul.

In our most vulnerable condition, the Lord speaks to us if we will listen. The Lord spoke to my mother in her weakness and confusion. He spoke to me in my brokenness and inadequacy.

One last thing… Celebrate birthdays!

Every day?

Why not?

* * *

Cheryl Schuermann, a career educator and literacy consultant, writes for children and adults. Her published books include *When the Water Runs: Growing Up with Alaska,* a memoir about her mother's childhood, and two books for children. Cheryl and her husband reside in Oklahoma where they enjoy living close to family.

16

IF ONLY IT HAD BEEN ME

BY STEPHANIE FRELONE

If only it had been me, I thought, watching a fireman pump my brother's chest in the backyard while my house crackled and blazed. In my disassociated state, the chaos of exploding windows, billowing smoke, and leaping flames felt as removed to me as a movie's special effects to a casual viewer. All I could think about was the attention Danny was going to get after this was over.

Danny was forever one-upping me, and this would be his best one yet. No one would want to hear about my boring old walk out of the house when they could hear about a dramatic rescue by a firefighter. With Danny's luck, he'd get his picture in the newspaper. If only we could have switched bedrooms that night like we had planned. If only we hadn't gotten into a dumb squabble at the last minute, prompting our mom to send us to our own rooms. All that glory could have been mine, if only it had been me.

If only it had been me, I thought, watching an endless procession of crying people file past a too-small casket. Danny was the prankster, the class clown, the kid with the mischievous grin who would take your television apart and not tell you until after he put it back together. How could all that fun and potential be gone from the world while I, the bratty kid sister, got to live? The only explanation I could accept was that God had made a serious mistake. Each day I lived from now on would be a day stolen from a grave that should have been mine.

If only it had been me, I thought four years later, sobbing on my bed and clutching a bottle of pills. I was now fourteen years old and living in my older sister's basement. Barely out of her own teens, Tania had become my legal foster parent after finding out my mom was living in her bedroom while I lived on dry cereal. A burden to my sister, and a cold comfort to my mother, my place in the world as one who shouldn't exist seemed solidified. If ever there was a time for me to change that, it was now.

The first pill tumbled down my throat, followed by another. Then another. Two more pills joined the procession. I stuck out my tongue to receive another.

Jesus.

The word flashed in my brain, stilling my hand.

A strange curiosity butted up against my despair. Why would the name Jesus come to me now, of all times? Determined to find out, I returned the pill bottle to my sister's medicine cabinet and replaced it with a Bible, flipping to the Gospel of John on a whim.

I spent the next two weeks poring over the New Testament and learning about the Jesus whose name had thwarted my suicide attempt. An alien sense of hope began to unfurl. For so long I'd lived in the valley of the shadow of Danny's death, and now here I was, learning about yet another death that had occurred in my stead. And from a willing sacrifice, no less—someone who knew me from the before the creation of the world! Was it possible that I wasn't just a cosmic clerical error? Would it be okay if I stopped being the wrong survivor and became more than a conqueror in Christ?

Buoyed by those thoughts, I sought a relationship with Jesus, praying during my walks to and from school and saturating myself in Scripture in my spare time. Before long, I felt led to seek out a church. Remembering the pastor who had officiated Danny's funeral, I made the hour-long trek from my sister's house to his church. Within the walls of that building, I became the kid sister in a new family—a family that my mom would come to join herself as God began to heal the wounds in her heart.

A year later, I sat at Danny's graveside for the first time, singing hymns to my God as I cried for my brother. At first all I could see was Danny's grave, but as time passed, I began to see other things. A jackrabbit hopped out from behind a nearby gravestone and locked eyes with me before bounding away. A double rainbow stretched above the sky. Though tears still dampened my face, I let myself smile, knowing that I was seeing those small mercies because I was exactly where I was meant to be. Knowing that I wanted to spend the rest of my life grateful for mercies I would have never known, if only it had been me.

* * *

Stephanie Frelone is a stay-at-home mother who lives in Lloydminster, Saskatchewan. In 2004, she graduated from Millar College of the Bible and married her best friend, with whom she has shared an amazing seventeen years. She is a longtime lover of stories and enjoys perusing them in many forms, whether by reading, writing, gaming, or participating in community theater.

17

FROST IN MY SOUL

BY EMMA BLOOR

I flew down his stairs without realizing why I was afraid. I just was. I rushed to the front door and, stepping up onto my nine-year-old tiptoes, reached for the catch.

"Don't you dare go out that door!" his voice yelled.

The door unlatched, and I froze obediently. Terry Frost met me at the door, not quite ready to let me go while my mother's voice called me from the street for dinner.

"Emma!" she called again, and this time twinged with panic. I wasn't hiding around the parked cars with my friends.

The third time, Terry growled and muttered under his breath. He straightened my clothes with a stern warning of "Never tell!" and pulled the front door open.

The three shouts from my mother saved me that day. I had run terrified from my neighbor's bedroom and was able to hear her at the door. She saved me, but the image of his orange curtains never left. They were silent seeds that grew in the darkness where nightmares were kept, and while the consequences of Terry's deeds flourished, I stayed in my little world, separated from people.

For thirty years, those curtains came to mind, and then so would the other things. For years, I denied he affected my relationships, my trust, and my ability to be intimate with anyone. Even God. That is, until the week that I was called for jury service to judge the sexual abuse of two sisters spanning decades. It provoked me. I was not okay. I had never been okay.

Although I tried to convince myself what he had done hadn't affected me, it had, and it took me vomiting out his evil deeds in the court restroom to realize it.

That night, I broke down with my husband beside me. Confessing the truth was tricky when I had kept it from him for fifteen years. I was afraid of his reaction, to me and to Terry. It would not be difficult for my husband to discover where he lived and enact the vengeance he surely felt on my behalf.

Mingled in with the confusion was Jesus, and in an instant, I felt no shame—it was not my fault, and Jesus still loved me. The presence of His Spirit grew and brought me peace.

Admitting the scar in my soul started the repairing process, and it released burdens I didn't know I carried. I gave them to the lover of my soul; to my Husband of husbands, Jesus, who had died to protect me; to the Holy God who healed and blessed me then prepared me for the next stage of the healing process.

Forgiveness.

"If Terry Frost came to church a born again, Jesus loving, Bible reading Christian, what would you do?" I heard the Lord ask.

It pushed me to consider it. I could leave my church and risk not attending another, doubting my faith because God forgave a child molester. Maybe I would force Terry out by telling the church what he had done. Could I destroy the reputation of a repentant sinner, ostracized for the evil he had done? Where would be the freedom in that for me, for him, or for the Spirit of God to work?

I would forgive and live.

My abuser was not saved, yet I forgave. Whatever he had done, I would not wish eternal separation from God and an emptiness for his soul. I prayed for him to know Jesus, to have conviction and understanding in what repentance truly meant to a tortured mind.

Forgiveness freed me; it did not excuse his actions. Forgiveness freed my soul-ties and loosened from the Lord blessings in abundance and a shalom to my heart. It brought strength, power, and love. God forgave me when I asked, why not an abuser? Seventy-times-seven, He pardoned a genuine seeker of the Lord. God forgave them. He saved in prisons every day.

I extended that love to my abuser because I knew what had led him. I was familiar with the unseen devices of the enemy, and the ability he had to warp and deceive. I extended love to my abuser because I knew only a fraction of his life—a year through the eyes of a child. Who had he been as a boy? Who were his parents? Had they hurt him? Had they abused him? Was this behavior normal to him, or was he always bad?

I shrugged. What did I know? Only that no repentant child of God escaped knowing the truth of what they had done, and what Jesus had done to wipe it clean. For me and for my abuser.

I chose to forgive, and live, and I have never been happier.

* * *

British author **Emma Bloor** renewed her passion for writing during the 2020 lockdown. It lifted her confidence to share experiences and life challenges. Her heart is to help people overcome soul-hurts and to show the joy Jesus brings when a soul surrenders and allows God to do the work.

18

THE SECRETS WE KEEP

BY LINDA L. KRUSCHKE

I carried a secret. Truth be told, I had buried more than one secret deep in my soul.

When I married my husband, he was unaware of the storm brewing deep in my heart and mind. I kept from him my secrets about the four times I'd been raped, and the abortion I had to erase all traces of the last time. They were in the past and not relevant to our wedded bliss.

Until my secrets became painfully relevant.

"Why are you crying again? What's wrong?" he asked.

"I don't know," was all I could say.

My secrets had poisoned my mind and I began my emotional retreat. Not consciously, but gradually, I sunk into myself. Flashbacks of being raped put me on edge. It began with a small flinch when he touched me or came up behind me to give me a loving embrace. This simple pulling away morphed into angry fits of rage over minor transgressions. Then came the bouts of uncontrollable sobbing. I still kept the truth to myself.

I tried many methods of overcoming my depression born of trauma. Drinking only made things worse. The academic success of law school only postponed the worst, a temporary band aid. Motherhood brought but a brief reprieve of veiled joy. Counseling and antidepressants provided only partial relief.

I believed I was destined to be forever broken and hopeless. It seemed unfair to put my husband and toddler son through a lifetime of despair shackled to my misery. So, I made a plan that involved all the pills in our medicine cabinet. I would enter a deep sleep and never awaken. We three would be free.

But God had other plans.

The day I lost my last glimmer of hope, I cried out to God. And "He heard my voice; He heard my cry for mercy" (Psalm 116:1b NIV). At the invitation of a friend, I attended my first Bible study since before the trauma that caused my depression. The women in the group showed me love and hope. They prayed for God to heal my depression. There was no miraculous overnight healing. It's not like one day I was depressed and the next day I wasn't. But He did answer their prayers in a miraculous way by giving me a dream about my first rapist asking to be forgiven. The dream was not God's first attempt to teach me that anger and unforgiveness fueled my misery, but it was the attempt that finally broke through my stubborn will.

I knew I couldn't do it alone. I prayed God would help me to forgive and He answered that prayer too. Once I set my transgressors free, I finally escaped from the prison of my own making. Light displaced the darkness of my soul. Joy replaced hopelessness.

Unforgiveness had bled into my relationships and life story. Learning to forgive stemmed my bitterness and revived the abundant life Jesus promised.

One in five women has experienced date rape. And it seems logical that we have a right to be angry. But if we cling to this right, unforgiveness will taint our relationships and steal our hope and joy. We owe it to ourselves to speak up, and then to forgive and trust God with eternal justice.

Sometimes my depression threatens to return, even decades after God's redemption. I can almost always trace it to a grudge I am harboring against someone—usually someone who is oblivious to the pain they caused. A couple of winters ago, I experienced deep depression as I hadn't felt in a long time. I snapped at my husband for any number of innocent comments. Tears sprang to my eyes without warning. I felt myself spiraling out of control. But God reminded me of the lesson of forgiveness I had learned so long ago. I stepped back and examined my heart. I discovered a grudge had taken root. Someone at work had wronged me and I needed to forgive.

Whenever I find myself on the brink of despair, God reminds me it is forgiveness that will keep me from tumbling into the abyss. He reminds me I can trust Him with meting out justice in His wisdom.

Are you struggling with feelings of despair, unable to forget some transgression you've tried to bury and forget? Ask God to help you bring your secret into the light. Acknowledge your anger, give it over to Him, and ask Him to help you forgive the person who hurt you, because "if the Son sets you free, you will be free indeed" (John 8:36 NIV).

* * *

Linda L. Kruschke writes candid memoir and fearless poetry. She aspires to show women that God's redemption and healing are just a story away. She blogs at AnotherFearlessYear.net and AnchoredVoices.com, and has been published in *Fathom Magazine*, *The Christian Journal*, *Bible Advocate*, iBelieve.com, WeToo.org's blog, *The Mighty*, and several anthologies.

19

RESCUED BY AN ANGEL

BY CECILIA JAMES

I grew up in a family marred by domestic violence, and by the time I was thirteen, my parents parted ways. I was then raised by my grandmother in a remote rural area while my mother worked her fingers to the bone trying to provide for us. When I finished high school, I was lucky to get a sponsor for my university studies, a ticket out of poverty.

However, with time, I lost my bearings. I got involved with a man I thought was "prince charming," who promised me heaven and the stars. At first, he was so loving, but he later started controlling how I dressed, which friends I spoke to and when. He subtly controlled all my movements so that no one noticed. He also had a roving eye, pursuing each dress that crossed his path, while I kept hoping he would change.

One day, I realized I was pregnant. I was shattered. Never in my life did I experience such conflicting emotions. Keeping the pregnancy meant I had to drop out of university as my sponsor was strict. Terminating the pregnancy was against my religion, culture, and every ounce of my beliefs. Dropping out was not an option, as I was my family's only hope.

After much anguish and countless sleepless nights, I

terminated the pregnancy with my partner's support. He changed for a short period and became the loving person I wished for. A couple of years later, I got pregnant again before completing my studies, and the same procedure applied, even though I was against it. However, my partner vowed that as soon as I graduated, we would have the wedding of our lives.

After graduation, when I was looking forward to the promised marriage, I realized that I was pregnant for the third time. He ordered me to abort, stating that he was not ready to be a father as he still needed to build his mother a house and send his siblings to school. For the first time in my life, my naive eyes opened.

I realized that he never had any intention of marrying me in the first place. This was a player who had perfected his craft through years of experience and had no conscience at all. To make matters worse, I had a distorted view of what love was due to my background, and I put up with a lot of abuse in the name of love. However, one thing was clear in my mind: I would not abort again. At first, my partner tried to use his tongue to soften me up, but my ears had developed thick wax. When he saw that talking was not helping, he became physically abusive, but I refused to budge. Then followed the humiliation of openly dating other girls to spite me, but I remained firm.

A dear friend of mine talked me back to church and encouraged me to find my way back to God. I honestly tried to repair my relationship with God, but I was in such a mess that it did not work out. I experienced serious mental health issues, and suicidal thoughts became my constant companion.

When I eventually gave birth to my child, I failed to bond with her. I was like a zombie—no emotions left. My mother took over the parenting role. When my daughter was a few months old, I left home for the city to look for a job. At least that part of my brain was still working. I got a high-paying job, but I did not forget what had happened to me.

I hated men with a passion, and in no time, I started my revenge mission of breaking as many hearts as possible. This nearly cost me my life. As I lay on a hospital bed recovering from a near-death experience, my friend came to see me. She was the only one who had not written me off like everyone else.

Upon discharge, she took me in—no questions asked, no judgment meted. I was penniless and homeless. She arranged for a job at one of the shelters for survivors of domestic violence. She did not stop there but lured me back to church. At first, I accompanied her as a sign of gratitude, but with time, God melted my heart. The good thing about reaching rock bottom is that you realize that the only way out is looking up to God.

When I look back at my life now, I am grateful for the experiences I encountered. Those encounters shaped me to be a stronger and better version of my former self. Most importantly, I revel in my role as an advocate for survivors of domestic violence.

* * *

Cecilia James is a social worker with extensive experience in family counselling and therapy. A woman after God's Word and principles, she is passionate about writing Christian articles and believes in telling authentic stories to inspire and uplift others. Born and raised in Zimbabwe, she now resides in South Africa.

20

PURPOSEFUL PAIN

BY SUSAN KING

*A*lthough currently a popular catchall word, *trauma* in its kaleidoscope of forms is very real. It not only damages the child, but if not healed it can devastate the life of the adult they become. Like a third-degree burn, the layers of the heart and mind are damaged so deeply that without faith, without the touch of God's hand leading one out of that dark forest of the night, it is nearly impossible to live the life that God purposed for His child.

At the age of five, my father decided we no longer needed to attend church, and so anything spiritual was removed from my life. Looking back, without this foundation I find it odd that every year at Christmas time I would gather up the manger from the family room, place it on my bedroom floor, lie on my stomach with legs dangling, and move the figures around to play "Jesus is born."

When I was thirteen, and television stations went off the air around 3:00 AM, without knowing why I would stay up all night just to hear Perry Como end that day's broadcast singing, "The Lord's Prayer." In this manner did God whisper to me.

As childhood rushed into adulthood, it was a whisper that

grew faint until I no longer heard it. A high school dropout, pregnant at sixteen, and married to a man twice my age, I became deaf to God's whisper as I struggled through a challenging marriage and life with an autistic child, and maintained three jobs in order to survive.

It was not until many years later, in 1993, did I again open myself to the whisper of God. I found it extraordinary that He knew me, knew my wounds so well that my salvation would not be my idea but His. He knew my feminine heart wanted to be pursued. He gave assurance that He came after *me*, and not the other way around. It is a profound experience to open the Word of God and find a verse that describes your relationship with Him, written out, thousands of years before you were born. Ten years into our relationship, I discovered Isaiah 65:1, "I revealed myself to those who did not ask for me, I was found by those who did not seek me."

My life did not spin into sugary clouds of happiness by joining into a union with God. There was so much pain to heal, so much trauma to confront, so much forgiveness that needed to flow from me—both forgiveness for those who had scarred me, and most difficult of all, forgiveness for myself. Although it sounds daunting, it took years of intentionally seeking God's peace, counseling, discovering grace for myself and others, workbooks, seminars, and journaling. But once I began to experience the benefits of these works, through volunteering I began to impart what I was learning to others who were seeking the same. This, for me, is the true purpose of pain and the sweetness of a life surrendered to God, for the discomfort is not in vain, nor wasted, if you heal from it and then use what you have learned to benefit those seeking peace.

Once when I was watching a well-known biblical teacher teaching lessons from Mary and Martha, I heard her say two words I would have never imagined together in a sentence. Those words seemed to stick to my soul and, without much

TRIUMPH FROM TRAGEDY

warning, began flying out of my pen in the form of what I have always referred to as a Holy Ghost poem, as no other explanation makes sense to me. I have used it in many classes to minister to others, and I share it with you here hoping you find comfort in reading it.

The Sweetest Gift

Of all the gifts I know our loving Father brings,
The answered prayers
Protection from all things unseen,
The peace within your heart
The small simplistic things,
That cry from deep within your soul
Will bring the greatest joy of all
He hears the anguish in your call
The sweetest gift there is of all
Is desperation.
When there is no place else to run
But to His grace
To fall upon your knees and seek His gentle face
There is no fear He does not know
No wound He cannot bind and so
The sweetest gift of all I know
Is desperation.
Sweet desperation brings you to your Father's throne
Surrender all and be assured you're not alone
In deepest, darkest hour of need
His light illuminates all things,
Come to Him broken and be healed
With His shed blood you have been sealed
Find comfort in His love so real
And know,
The sweetest gift of all is desperation.

***

Susan King has written for her own pleasure for many years and has only recently begun to explore publishing her works. Although her poem "The Sweetest Gift" was published years ago on Christianity.com, she is continuing to develop her gifts and is currently working on a memoir.

21

MY RESENTMENT DISAPPEARED

BY CHIZOBAH MARY ALINTAH

*B*itter is life to be sweet. A taste of life's bitterness before its sweetness is a taste of life to its fullest.

As a child, I grew up with a father, a mother, sisters, and a brother. But as an adult, it's like I never had a father or a brother despite the closeness families share living together as one. Like a stranger I lived with them.

My dad, who was supposed to be my builder, was my destroyer. He watched me grow and left me destroyed. His greed blinded his eyes, and he sold me like a product to be purchased. My happiness mattered not. My brother, who was supposed to be my shield, supported my father: "Like father, like son."

Being disappointed by my own family, I extended my trust to my extended family. But unknown to me, they were all the same. The uncle I went to stay with was a replica of my dad. Living with him was like living with a monster. I was a servant to him and to his friends. There was no breathing space to be myself. He stripped me of my teenhood, just like my dad stripped me of my childhood. As he tried to stop my education to make me a full-time servant, I decided to leave his home. I became a wanderer.

I searched for a father, a brother, an uncle in every man I came across. But I was so naïve to detect the beast in them all, and they played me like a football. I vowed never to trust men again. But the unexpected happened that made me go back on my word and give them a second chance.

Out of the blue, he came like an angel, he the breadwinner of my family—my cousin. I fondly called him "my angel," but he turned out to be a wolf in human clothing among all the men born of a woman that I have ever known. He had an evil agenda behind his goodwill. He nearly forced himself on me, but I escaped. This shattered me into pieces and left me with the option of committing suicide because I had no one to run to, not even my mother.

This affected my relationship with men to the extent I distanced myself from them like they were oceans where I would drown. My dream of getting to know and feel the friendship of the opposite sex was aborted. I couldn't give in to any relationship. The bitter experience I had had with my family made me always expect the worst from any male I came in contact with. I couldn't let anyone in. I became a father and brother to myself.

Haunted by the experience with men, I became depressed and dejected with a probing question. I asked my mother, "Why me?" If my sisters have no problem with men, she said, "It is your fate—deal with it! We all have life's battle, there's nothing I can do." Then it dawned on me that my fate is in my hands. Not even my birth mother who brought me into this world could be called my savior.

The word "savior" knocked me out and into a trance. I realized how foolish I had been to put all my trust in men, thinking they could give me the internal peace I sought to be at peace with myself. But I was mistaken. All through my growing up, I thought that because I never had a beautiful relationship with my dad, my adulthood would be ugly. But with the help of the Holy Spirit, my eyes were opened to the greater "HE" who will never disappoint me, even if all the men of this planet Earth disappointed me and left me dejected like an alien.

The Almighty God will not. After all, He sent His only begotten Son from heaven to die on earth for the whole world. Can't He also save me? If only I can believe and put all the trust I had put in men on Him, then I'll have the Savior I seek and be at peace with life.

I awoke from the trance. Like a ghost, my resentment towards men disappeared, and I surrendered all to the Savior Jesus Christ, the Son of the Almighty He. And He became the lover of my life, filling me with all the love I was deprived of by all the men I ever came across.

* * *

Chizobah Mary Alintah is a freelance writer, poet, and journalist. She has been working as a freelance writer for over two years. Her journalistic writing exposes her to many topics on the happenings of life. You may learn more about her services on all social media. She writes under the name "Chichi Alintah."

22

THE PRUNING

BY JESSICA GALLANT

At sixteen, I made the worst mistake of my life. I left home, wanting to do things my way and have freedom from parental authority. Three short years later, I was the teenage mother of two children under the age of one and a half, their father only around half the time. I had no regrets having the children, nor do I now, but it was not what I had envisioned for my life, and much less as one coming from a Christian home. Before I knew it, my abusive relationship fell apart, and I was on my own with two babies.

Shortly after that, I was deemed mentally unstable, producing instability even in our living conditions. With that pronounced over my life, my children were taken from me. It was the hardest situation I have ever had to go through. Though I had disgraced my family, and caused incalculable heartbreak, my parents stepped in and took in my children from the foster care system.

It was a long time of healing ahead. I had to work on my life and do a rapid grow-up and 180-degree change. It felt impossible. It didn't matter how hard I tried, I was merely shining the outside of a dark, sinful, and depressive life. I married my husband, and though this brought stability in my floundering life and a companion I needed, it was not the transformation I needed. It was only after a decade that the Lord laid hold on my life and worked on me from the inside out. Once I submitted to Him, He changed and perfected me in the ways I could not on my own. I'm not perfect, but I know I am changed and righteous in Him.

My pruning was far from over. Just as I was a brand-new creation in Christ, continuing on the paths of righteousness, I was becoming a better person through Him for myself and my children. But, my life, and that of my children, shattered once more when we received news that their father was found dead of an overdose in his apartment.

Through this tragedy, Jesus kept my once wobbling mind! Praise God! God worked through these trials, strengthening me, purging me, stabilizing me, maturing me, and holding me fast as He worked upon me. I was, and still am, on the Potter's wheel. I am learning to wait and trust in Jesus. He is my Stay.

John wrote that when my heart condemns me, He is greater than my heart! I have learned in these various trials, starting the day my children left me, that He is my completion. Abiding in Him, He will work all things together for good—my good—and His glory. Were I not subjected to these fiery trials, I could not say without question that the Lord is my Deliver, my Keeper!

At the moment of this writing, I am just over a week away from being with my children again. Our relationship is close and endearing despite my sin. All praise and glory to Him who can do abundantly overall we can ask or think. I know that He does all things well. If it had been my timing, or had this not happened to our family, I would be in sin and teaching my children—even if just through my actions—sinfulness.

But thanks be to God, I cannot only daydream anymore, or simply lead my children to Jesus on Skype, but I will one day be able to fulfill the role of motherhood—raising my children in the fear and admonition of the Lord. It's nothing I have done, even in this, but to be patient and submit. It's been all of His great mercy to me. Oh, for grace to trust Him more!

To sum up this little life story, I would encourage you, broken, damaged, imperfect mother, to find your rest and hope in God, to submit to Him until it's no longer you who live, but Christ who lives in you. I would encourage you to endure the fiery trials. In due time, I do believe that perfect purification will come forth. Trust in the God who said He will redeem the years that were stolen, those which the cankerworm ate. Bless God for He is the God who forgives even the foolishness of our youth that He might be feared.

*　*　*

Jessica Gallant is an indie author on Amazon. She's been saved, baptized in Jesus' name, and filled with the Holy Ghost. She writes nonfiction, YA historical fiction, and children's books. A Canadian mom of teens, Jessica loves Christ, her husband, her kids, elephants, cats, and her Acadian heritage.

23

THE RARE GIFT

BY KRISTIN FAITH EVANS

Her heart rate's dropping! Why aren't they doing anything?

The beeping slowed. 100...80...60...40...20. Her heart went silent.

Oh God, please save her.

The bed clicked below me. The doctors raced me down the hall to the operating room. A woman ran beside my head. "She's going to be okay. You're going to be okay."

I want to believe her. I have to believe her.

A man switched my oxygen to a large anesthesia mask. "Here, breathe deeply." The candy smell of the gas lured me.

How can I wake up not knowing? God, please, please let her be okay. Save ...

* * *

"She doesn't have it!"

I pried open my eyes.

Who's this woman standing at the foot of my bed? Who doesn't have what?

"She doesn't have the fatal heart condition! Your daughter's okay. She's doing well!"

What? It just vanished? Oh God, thank you! She's a miracle!

I felt my husband squeezing my hand.

"But your daughter *does* have a rare genetic disorder, different from your son's. This syndrome is much more severe. It's called Cri du chat syndrome."

These four words would forever change my life.

I've lost my typical baby girl. I'll never have a normal life like other moms. God, why? I just want a healthy baby. You've given us the gift of Bethany Grace though.

* * *

I waited as Bethany Grace endured two rounds of surgeries. I watched her stop breathing. I pleaded with God as doctors performed CPR on my angel. Then, I gasped when she miraculously revived after their efforts had failed. At three months old, she came home from the NICU. But the overwhelming stress stole my excitement. I labored to love and care for both my son and medically fragile baby who lay hooked up to four machines around the clock. I relived the traumatic pregnancy over and over.

My marriage is crumbling. The strain is tearing us apart. I can't keep going like this. I'm losing myself. Unraveling.

I spiraled deeper into a dark crisis of faith and a dangerous depressive episode.

How could God be good and allow my innocent baby to suffer? Watch our family go through this pain and do nothing? God, where are you?

A dozen depression medications, fifteen months of therapy, marriage counseling, and two psychiatric hospitalizations came crashing down. Slipping from my family's grasp, I made a lethal suicide attempt.

***

As if exiting a tunnel, I heard muffled voices. I opened my eyes to doctors in white coats surrounding my bed. "You've survived on a ventilator for four days. By all medical accounts, you shouldn't have survived. We can't explain it. You're very lucky."

I've been given a second chance. God, please forgive me! Thank you for saving me!

But returning home from the hospital to the same pressure cooker of stress, I still faced seemingly impossible circumstances.

I don't know how to truly live.

"Kristin, what options do you have?" My therapist's question helped me realize that I had three choices: I could continue to fight against reality and be miserable, I could attempt again to escape by death, or I could fully dive into my new life as a mother of two children with profound special needs.

Standing on a shimmering lakeshore, I embraced the beautiful mystery of faith. "God, I don't understand how You could allow suffering and still be good. But I release the need to find the answer. I trust You."

I'm choosing life once and for all. I'm giving it everything I have left. But there's no magic fix for my depression. I'm going to defy the stigma. I'm no longer ashamed for people to know about my intensive mental health treatment.

I began my challenging road to recovery, which led me to hard work in therapy, meds, and mending relationships. Joy and deep meaning flourished in the most unexpected place—there in the midst of my heartache and trials. Embracing my painful circumstances freed me to truly begin living. Rising up out of hopelessness, I fully recovered from my mental illness, grew deeper in my faith, rescued my marriage, and helped my children thrive. Through sharing in my children's challenges and living through their serious illnesses, I discovered one of the greatest gifts in life: waking up each morning with simple gratitude for the new day.

But I don't want my pain to have just been about me.

I returned to graduate school to become a licensed therapist. I've grown passionate about empowering others with this message: "God's waiting to help you. He cares for you deeply. He wants you to be healthy and whole. Other people are waiting to help you. There's no shame in seeking professional help. Don't suffer in silence any longer. Hope and joy are on the horizon if you are willing to journey there."

* * *

Kristin Faith Evans's passion is journeying with others to deeper faith and emotional healing. With her MSSW and MA in Christian Education, she is experienced in various ministries, Christian counseling, couples therapy, and crisis counseling. She lives with her husband and two children in Nashville, TN. Follow Kristin at www.SpecialNeedsMomsBlog.com and www.InspiringWordsfortheJourney.com.

24

JONATHAN DAVID

BY HOWARD ABRAMS

Mid-January of 1982 is more than half a lifetime ago. Becky and I were young and ready to start our family. Becky was pregnant with our first child, due in May, but there were complications. Becky had a condition called placenta previa (the baby was attached too low on the uterus). She had to restrict her activities in hopes she could carry the baby full term. A major ice storm had hit Birmingham, shutting down the city. Over the weekend of January 16 and 17, the ice began to melt. That Sunday, Becky began having back pains. She called her doctor. He told her to come in early Monday.

That Monday, as we drove toward her doctor's office, Becky went into labor. The traffic was slow moving, and we realized we would not make it in time. We were near Brookwood Hospital, so we turned into their emergency room lot. The attendants realized what was happening and took Becky immediately. After what seemed like an eternity (but really only fifteen minutes), our son was born. Unfortunately, he came far too early. He was tiny, weighing one pound, three ounces.

The ER doctor said Brookwood was not prepared to care for such a tiny newborn. University Hospital, two miles away, had a newborn intensive care unit. Our son was transported there by ambulance. Becky's parents had arrived, and they took her to their house while I followed the ambulance.

The next morning, we went to see our son, Jonathan David, at the hospital. The doctor in charge of the unit explained his situation. Jonathan was in the best place possible. This was the only hospital in the area equipped to treat such tiny infants. But in 1982, at twenty-four weeks, a baby could not survive for long outside the womb. While Jonathan was perfectly normal for his developmental age, he would have to be ventilated to survive. However, the process destroyed new lung tissue as it developed. The doctor told us that very few infants born at twenty-four weeks survived, and he encouraged us to make funeral plans.

We were on an emotional roller coaster for the next few months. The ups and downs depended on Jonathan's medical news. I was on the downside one morning at work. A coworker noticed and asked what was wrong. I told her, and she shared the words of Psalm 121 with me. I learned that God never sleeps nor slumbers and is never surprised. I did not have to worry constantly about Jonathan, for God knew and cared.

At six months of age, Jonathan weighed what a full term two-month-old baby would weigh, but he still needed the ventilator. We developed a routine: go to work, visit Jonathan, and go home. One night, we were tired and went to bed early. We were roused when the phone rang. A nurse told us a piece of Jonathan's equipment had failed. An alarm should have alerted the nurses but did not. It was a busy night. By the time someone noticed Jonathan, he was turning blue. They tried to revive him, but he did not respond. We drove frantically to the hospital but when we arrived, Jonathan was dead. His brave fight for life was over.

Our pastor preached the funeral. He had experienced similar sadness. He had lost one child as a toddler, and another was stillborn. He was a great comfort for us, as were friends and family who prayed for us throughout.

God healed us. We decided to try again. In 1983, Becky became pregnant. The baby's due date was Valentine's Day. Becky's doctor was cautious, but this time the pregnancy went smoothly. On January 18, about a month before the predicted due date, Becky had a morning doctor's appointment. His office was near my workplace, so I dropped her off and went to work. I had been there about an hour when I got a call. Becky was in the early stages of labor. I left work for the hospital, located next to her doctor's office. That evening, Becky gave birth to a beautiful baby girl. Even though she was a month earlier than the predicted due date, she was full-term.

God took away the sting out of January 18. From now on, we would remember it not only as the beginning of Jonathan's tragic life, but of our daughter's.

Jonathan's life inspired me. First, Jonathan, who had little chance of living, fought for life to the end. I can fight passionately for things I believe in. Second, when I read Psalm 121, I recall my kindly co-worker. When we see those who are struggling or discouraged, we should do what we can to encourage them. We may never know the long-term effects of our words on others.

* * *

Howard Abrams was born in Cairo, Georgia, before he moved to Hoover, Alabama. He attended Ramsay High School (1964) and Samford University (1968). He is retired from the Social Security Administration. Abrams is married to Frances King Abrams. He has two children, Jonathan David Abrams, deceased, and Katherine Abrams Gray, of Salem, Virginia.

25

ZOE KARIS

BY HAYDEN WALKER, 1ST PLACE WINNER

"*I* have some concerns." The words echoed in the exam room. My hands grasped my swollen belly as I felt my baby flutter inside. The floral painting hanging on the wall seemed to be the only anchor in my world that had suddenly turned upside down. The obstetrician whisked my husband and me down the elevator to the office of a Maternal-Fetal Medicine specialist, where we learned our unborn child was very sick.

I had anticipated the day's appointment with great excitement. Until that defining moment, I naively thought the most important information we would hear that day was the gender of our firstborn. We did learn that God had given us a daughter. We also learned that the specialist suspected our daughter had an extremely rare skeletal disorder. He rattled off a long word as the name of this condition, which I couldn't understand. I didn't ask for clarification though, partly from shock and partly because I saw the sonographer write it down on a sticky note for me.

We left the office in a daze. On the drive home, I remembered the sticky note inscribed with our daughter's diagnosis. I pulled it out of my purse and stared at it in disbelief. Written on that brightly colored square of paper were the words *Thanatophoric Dysplasia*. I felt an iron clamp come around my lungs as I gasped to my husband, "Thanatos!"

In seminary, I had studied the Greek language. I immediately recognized *thanatos* as the Greek word meaning death. Our daughter's proposed diagnosis included the word death. It felt like more than I could bear. I stared out the window and wondered how the world was still moving as mine seemed to be standing still.

And yet in those moments of utter brokenness, my faith in God anchored me to truth. Although death—*thanatos*— was her diagnosis, her destiny because of Christ is life. *Zoe* is the Greek word for life. As such, we named our daughter Zoe Karis. Saying her name became an act of hope, a proclamation that Jesus conquered the grave for her, and for us. *Thanatos* may seem to rule in this world, but it is not the final word. Because of Christ, *zoe* is our promised inheritance.

As the months passed following Zoe's diagnosis, I read and studied the Bible like it was oxygen. I had believed the doctrine of the bodily resurrection, but as life and impending death wiggled in my womb, I became captivated by the beauty of the glorious hope that is ours in Christ. I had believed with my head, but now I believed with the deepest parts of my heart.

On a warm June morning, three months after that heart-wrenching day of diagnosis, the veil between heaven and earth became quite thin. Our beautiful Zoe Karis was born and went onward to heaven. Our great sorrow was met by the insurmountable peace and presence of the Holy Spirit. When that dreaded day came, the clouds that had been gathering for months were pierced by light.

I was reminded of Noah's pattern of faith and obedience. He did not begin construction on his ark after the rain began to fall. Before the clouds gathered in the sky, Noah gathered the cypress wood and pitch. When the floodwaters rose, Noah was buoyed by the ark and by his faith in God. The same was true for me. God gave grace to keep me afloat as the Spirit reminded me of truth gathered up in prior months.

My heart was struck down as we chose the wood for Zoe's casket instead of her crib, yet I remembered that Jesus is not unfamiliar with wood. He hung upon the cross to defeat the power of death. I look to that old rugged cross and see Jesus' victory for us in His suffering. His suffering means that my suffering is laced with hope. The days were not without deep pain, but I found that sound doctrine was my ark.

It has now been five years since our beloved Zoe Karis died. Her life and death shook our whole world. And yet, as everything came crashing down, what we believed about God didn't change. In fact, the doctrines that we believed only became dearer. I found that the substance of what we believe really matters. What we believe about the doctrines of God, sin, and suffering shape the lenses through which we understand our experiences. It is vital to establish a sturdy theological ark, doing the work of building your faith, plank by plank, truth by truth. When the storms of life come, which they inevitably will, it is only the truth of God himself as revealed in Scripture which is sturdy enough to keep your ark above the waters.

* * *

Hayden Walker is a Bible teacher passionate about accessible, expositional preaching. A graduate of Beeson Divinity School, she was the recipient of the James Earl Massey Preaching Award. Hayden works with the Robert Smith Jr. Preaching Institute at Beeson. She and her husband live in Arkansas, raising Zoe's little brothers.

26

A WOMAN FORSAKEN

BY STEPHANIE RODDA

*I*t was Autumn 1993. I sat on the front porch of our home and faced deep disappointment once again. I felt betrayed by my own body, misunderstood by the people I loved the most, and abandoned by God.

My husband, Henry, and I had been married a decade. We were childless. The first and second year of our marriage we experienced pregnancy but lost those babies before they came to full term. While I was comforted that we would see them in eternity, my arms remained empty.

We had tried to give it time and let nature take its course for a few years. We had tried old wives' tales, herbal remedies, temperature taking, chart keeping, several laparoscopic procedures to address the endometriosis, and even a round of fertility pills. We had prayed prayers, been anointed, claimed verses, stood in faith, and as a show of how sure I was, I had given up my job in preparation for the baby I was sure we would soon have.

Those who cared for me tried their best to comfort me. While I appreciated their efforts, I felt alone in my despair. They did not understand what I was facing. They could not relate. They did not know.

I had taken my Bible out on the porch with me, and I stared at its pages blankly. Desperate for understanding and longing for direction, I tried to focus on the words printed on the delicate pages. I couldn't. I squeezed my eyes tightly shut, willing away the unbidden tears and allowed myself to pour out my emotion through swirling thoughts in my mind. Obviously, God did not feel I would be a good mother. I must be incapable of that kind of love and commitment. I had failed to give Henry a child; surely, he was disappointed in me. I was faulty, broken, not enough.

There was no holding back the tears now, they streamed freely. I sat down the untouched coffee and reached for a tissue. My Bible began to slip off my lap, and I instinctively grabbed for it. I embraced it and held it close to my broken heart. "Help me God! Please help me! If this is not Your will for me then please take away this desire, this longing, this emptiness! Please help me understand!"

I drew the Bible from my chest and let my eyes fall upon the page that had been revealed as I had rescued it from falling. For the rest of my days, as long as I draw breath, I will never forget that moment, those words.

"The Lord has forsaken me, the Lord has forgotten me" (Isaiah 49).

I could scarcely believe what I was reading. Great hope did not abound that morning; instead, a trickle of hope coursed its way into my aching heart. I didn't understand everything, and all the pain was not erased instantly. But I knew my God had heard me and answered my cry for help. I knew there was a purpose in the delay. I knew a plan was in place. I was not forgotten.

From that moment I began to seek diligently what God had in store for us rather than my own plans. It took several months to unfold before we found ourselves enrolled in the required training classes to becomes state licensed foster parents. Many considered us foolish as they cautioned that we were setting ourselves up for heartbreak. Henry was very hesitant at first, worried that the pain of letting go would be too much for me. I addressed all the worries and concerns with a newfound determination. I had been called. I would answer the call.

When people asked how I could do such a thing, I asked them, how could I not? What this could do to me was not as important as what this could do for a hurting child who may be feeling just as abandoned and forgotten as I had felt.

We fostered for fifteen years. Dozens of children came into our lives and into our homes. Some stayed for short times, some for years, and seven stayed forever as we were blessed to adopt them. Throughout those years, God met me many more times in the pages of Scripture with comfort and strength to do what He had asked me to do. Those stories I will leave for another day.

I hope you will today take this one thing with you. The Word of God, and what He says, is more real than what you see or hear or feel. I know this to be true. I have lived it.

Exactly as the Word proclaimed, I had hoped in Him, and I was not disappointed.

* * *

Stephanie Rodda is a freelance and devotional writer, author, blogger, inspirational speaker, wife and adoptive mother, Christ-follower, and student of the Word of God.

27

FROM DEVASTATION TO GRACE

BY PATRICIA SIMMONS TAYLOR

May 18, 1981, is forever stamped in my family's soul. Eight years earlier, we had moved to a rural area so our three sons could have more freedom and safety. Our boys rode dirt bikes in the woods, and they were good at it. We stressed safety and insisted on the use of helmets as well as following safety rules while riding. Jeff, the eldest, worked after class at the school he had attended since first grade. He asked for a street bike so he would have his own transportation to and from school. We were against it at first but finally agreed. He offered to help pay for the bike and buy the gas. He got his license, and we bought him a regulation helmet. Jeff's dad, A.L., took him out and rode with him, warning him of the dangers facing a motorcyclist.

That morning, as Jeff approached the school, a teacher did not see him coming and turned left in front of him. His motorcycle struck her car, and his body was thrown into the air. His helmet came off and his head hit the pavement with no protection. By this time, I arrived to take our other two sons to school. To our horror, Jeff was lying in the road, the motorcycle next to him. His helmet, still fastened, was in the ditch.

Paramedics arrived and a medical helicopter was called to take him to a major trauma hospital in the area. The doctors there didn't know if he would survive since his eyes were set and dilated. Jeff was not breathing. He was in a deep coma, and it looked hopeless.

The terrible memory of his bruises and swollen head will always be with us. Our Christian faith and belief in the power of prayer gave us hope. I knelt in the waiting room and begged God to help him. Within a day, he could squeeze our hand when asked. Like a flower opening up, he responded a bit more every day. It was twenty-one days before he spoke. Every word gave us happiness! Therapy began, but he was in the ICU for twenty-eight days and remained helpless. He could not walk or even sit up.

On June 26, he was transferred to a rehabilitation hospital for more extensive therapy. He responded well to it and was finally able to go home on July 23, 1981. His initial recovery took sixty-five days. We were happy to have him back home, but the real work was about to begin, not only physically but mentally and emotionally. A psychologist and other doctors continued his care. He had a homebound teacher when school started back. He did well but wanted to be with his friends and classmates. Finally, he was able to go back to school.

The next two years of Jeff's recovery were rewarding in many ways but also difficult for our family. The brain damage was permanent, yet we still had hope because the doctors told us that every year he lived, improvement would occur. We held onto that and prayed our way through it. Jeff saw a neuropsychologist on November 22, 1983, receiving a good report. He went to bed that night, seemingly fine, but a bit tired. I kissed him goodnight and told him I loved him. He said he loved me, too, and asked me to tell his dad, who had gone to bed earlier, that he loved him, too, and for him to be careful going to work the next morning. I went to bed, leaving the door to Jeff's room open.

The next morning, I woke A.L. and fixed his lunch. We had a rescue cat that we had raised on a bottle, but he wasn't in the kitchen. A.L. went to Jeff's room to see if the cat was in there with him and to check on Jeff. The horrible way he cried out my name, I knew something was terribly wrong. I ran to Jeff's room, but we knew he was gone. One of our other sons tried to give him CPR, but it was too late. The Lord had come and taken Jeff to heaven. One might wonder how this could be called a triumph in such a loss. Jeff had accepted the Lord just a few years earlier, so even though the situation didn't end as we hoped, we knew where Jeff was. Best of all, we know we will see him again.

Since then, A.L. has also gone on to be with the Lord. Jeff and his dad are back together, waiting for the rest of us. The joy of our reunion will truly be a blessing like no other!

* * *

Patricia Simmons Taylor began writing during childhood. Her motto is, "Writing to Give Others Hope." It is her prayer that her work will lead readers to Jesus. She is currently working on a book, *The Grace of a Sparrow*, and her additional current titles can be found on Amazon.

28

TRUSTING GOD THROUGH IT ALL

BY TRACY RIGGS

I will never forget that night. My husband left to pick up a video for a relaxing night at home.

While he was gone, I reminisced. After going back to college and getting a master's degree, I was finally employed within my career. After years of living anywhere we could rent affordably, we finally bought a house and flipped it, making it what we wanted. After years of hoping, praying, and even enduring fertility testing, we finally had a daughter who we loved very much and thanked God for every day.

Life was good.

While waiting for his return, my mood suddenly changed. I was on the bed playing with our daughter when I suddenly sensed something was wrong. No matter what I did, I couldn't shake the feeling.

I pinned it down to our relationship. I thought it was fine. Until I felt that strange impression, I wasn't worried about *us*.

When my husband got home, I asked if we could talk. I told him about this weird feeling and waited for his reassurance.

His next seven words rocked my world and changed it forever.

"I don't love you and never have."

I couldn't breathe. I didn't understand. There were no indications that anything had changed. We had been married over ten years. This doesn't "just happen."

I argued with him about his love for me. I told him that it didn't matter, that I would never agree to a divorce. I prayed desperately for God to intervene and fix this.

This couldn't happen to me. I was so sure we would stay together forever that I remembered joking early in our marriage that I would "kill him before I ever divorced him." Finally understanding that it never was funny, it hurt me to the core to think about my confidence then.

Over the next few years, I tried everything I could think of to save our marriage. I set up couples' counseling (he never thought the counselors were good enough); I signed us up for a marriage retreat (he thought the information didn't pertain to us); I talked to an older couple who mentored us on other matters (he thought that they didn't understand him).

I prayed and fasted and cried so much to God that I almost ran out of tears. I found appropriate Scripture and trusted those promises. I talked to other couples who had been married longer. I read books on marriage and took their advice.

We separated anyway.

I learned a lesson concerning free will. *Nothing* that a person does can make another change. God won't make a person change. I needed to trust God with my own life and let him go.

Time passed. He wouldn't do what it took to reconcile, and after initially being so adamant about wanting a divorce, he also wouldn't file.

Ironically, my desire to be in ministry motivated me to be the one to file for divorce. As far back as I could remember, I wanted to be an ordained minister. When an opportunity arose to do the coursework during our separation, I knew it was the right time. I finished the training and then asked about the ordination ceremony.

The answer floored me. I wasn't eligible to be ordained because I was separated. Single, married, or even divorced would have been fine.

I was none of these.

I realized I had tried everything in my power and had asked for God's intervention to save our marriage. I put in the time and hard work to become ordained. But there was nothing that I could do to make either situation have the outcome I wanted.

I spent lots of time thinking about what I learned—that God won't override one's choices and decisions, even if they rip apart another's world—and I applied that lesson. First, I surrendered my dream to be ordained. Then, I prayed until I found peace, and I filed.

It's been almost twenty years since that horrible night. I thought that God would quickly bring me a wonderful husband and stepdad for my young daughter. That didn't happen. I assumed He would provide another way to become ordained. This also didn't happen.

But God provided all I needed. I found an amazing house in my budget. He gave me the confidence, independence, and strength to be a single mom. I enjoyed the support of friends, family, and my church.

And then four years ago, as a bonus, He even brought me the wonderful man I prayed for those many years before.

Though it was never easy, God has been there whenever I've needed Him. Life might be difficult and people might make choices you don't agree with, but know that you can trust God *through it all.*

Life is still good.

***

Tracy Riggs is a freelance photographer and writer, with more than fifty articles and hundreds of photos published. Tracy is also an advocate for those with mental and physical illnesses and/or addictions and shares that message through posts at www.SpotlightonStigma.com.

Her website, www.NovelPhotos.com, includes her photography, writing, and blog information.

29

THE LONG ROAD BACK TO ME

BY SUSAN DEITZ SHUMWAY

I'm sitting alone in a very quiet house. The glow of the fireplace and the crackle of aged wood is all that I hear. As I stare into the fire, there is something mesmerizing about it. Stillness fills my space, and the only movement is the height of the flames and the cinders falling through the grate to their final resting place. My eyes are transfixed on the fire, and there is no movement in my chair except the beat of my heart and the steady movements of each silent breath causing the up and down methodical movements of my chest.

I am alone, and yet there is a comfortable, calm demeanor in my body and in my spirit. As I sit there, a peace envelopes me. It tells me I did the right thing, and the peace of God is present. But how can this be? Wasn't it just yesterday I was married, and there was life in our house? Yes, there was life, but it wasn't yesterday. It was nine years ago that I made the hardest decision of my life and left a bitter, abusive marriage to reclaim my life, my sanity, and my peace.

Well-meaning Christian friends were there to say, "Marriage is forever," "You don't jump ship, you NEVER jump ship," and "God will give you grace." All of these comments were made by well-meaning people. However, the pain was so deep, the pain so intense that my very will to live was being depleted faster than the seconds on a stopwatch are counted off.

And so I prayed, very earnestly, asking God to help me survive the marriage. Maybe if I prayed more, pretended things were tolerable, got more counseling. Instead, I found myself deeper in the reality that things would never change. Was this my cross to bear? Was God pleased with this relationship?

I knew in my heart the answer that was hard to face. Couple's counseling gave me temporary comfort, but it was always short-lived. It was *her* fault, *she* was giving up and we need to finish what we started, was her spouse's response. But there was no accountability or responsibility for his actions personally. *She* just needed to shape up.

And so, with a heavy heart, I moved out. I was dying inside and was left with nothing but empty promises and accusations. Watching the fire, I was reminded of how I felt. Just like someone trying to escape from a burning building, I knew the smoke was filling the room, the oxygen was being depleted every second, and I needed to do my best to escape while I was still able. Seconds of hesitation could possibly cost me my life, and so I fled. I frantically searched for a window or door, anything to get me the freedom I needed—a breath of fresh air. I felt my lungs would collapse. "Oh God, give me a breath of fresh air."

As I felt for the doorknob and grasped onto it with all my strength, it opened. I ran out as quickly as my body would allow me, and after a short distance, I collapsed on the lawn. I could feel the heat of the burning building as I laid there, but the distance between me and that building assured me that I was safe and out of harm's way.

I had escaped! My heart was pounding, and all the strength I had was now scattered between me and the building. But I was safe. So now what? Could I ever stand up by myself? Could I manage life alone? Questions pummeled me like popcorn in an air popper, flying in every direction, covering me with doubts and fears. I had no choice now, I must do this, even if it was the reality of a life alone. I realized that despite the ashes and broken dreams that were scattered around me, God had me in His hand, and there would be much greater things ahead than I had ever imagined. I have learned how God can take shattered dreams and a willing heart, mixed with complete dependence on Him, to make me beautiful in His sight. My desire is to look back and reflect on a never-failing God, and what He can do with a heart that says, "I am Yours."

I have learned that God is with us regardless of what we have done, and what others may do to us. He is God in the good times, and He is God in the bad times. I feel my worst day with God is still a good day.

* * *

Susan Deitz Shumway is a follower of Christ. Her joy has been seeing God work in her life. Her favorite thing in life is being a mom of two children who have added to her joy with beautiful spouses and six amazing grandchildren. Writing was born through her sorrow. She is in the process of writing her story, hoping she can bring comfort to others in the battle of abuse in marriage.

30

DESPAIR TO REPAIR

BY CHERYL GORE POLLARD

*D*ivorce. Such an ugly, devastating word. One I'd said I'd never contemplate, yet there I was, after ten years of marriage, seriously bumping the "D" word around in my head.

It wasn't that I'd suddenly given up. For two years I'd prayed and waited on God's answer. I wanted Him to hurry up and say, "Hey, go ahead. Do what you gotta do," but I knew He didn't work that way. I prayed, "If my husband can change, let me help him. If it is me, God, help me change." I tried to be better, do more, and work harder.

Things stayed much the same. My children and I walked on eggshells. Our home wasn't a home. God wanted me to make a decision based on faith, but I was embarrassed and afraid. How could divorce be a good thing? What would people think? With only a high school education, how could I provide?

I didn't realize faith must overcome fears.

Times worsened. Sometimes while driving, I'd meet a big rig and think, *just a nudge of the steering wheel and I'd be* …. Or maybe I could drive off a high embankment. God showed me I had to be strong during weakness. He made His presence perfect by placing images of my children, parents, and loving community members in my mind. I couldn't let them down. But lack of faith, the sly whisper of the Devil, and fear of "what if" was so frightening.

One afternoon, as I was driving, beside the road stood Miss Nora, a true woman of God, gathering her mail. God spoke. "Pull into the driveway. Miss Nora is there for you." I did, and we talked. She helped me understand God's all-powerful love for me and my family. She assured me He wouldn't leave me, and she assured me of His blessings if I put Him first. I'm sure God timed that meeting just for me.

I thought I'd kept my unhappiness and feelings of unworthiness hidden, but my immediate family and church family knew. What I didn't know was how hard they were praying for me and lifting me up before God. I was literally wrapped in love by those I love.

Meanwhile, my husband left the state to work. At last, I had "home" with no arguing, worry, or fear of physical retaliation for some little thing I'd done—or not done. God and I communicated. I grew in faith.

During one of my husband's once a week phone calls, he commented that changes were going to be made in our marriage.

Yes! I thought. *My prayers were heard*!

He went on, and my heart broke. "There will be changes," he said, "but not by me. You will be the one who makes them." I hung up the phone. All energy drained from me and I knew, without a doubt, God used that conversation to point me in the direction I should go.

I saw a divorce lawyer that week.

Meanwhile, I was elected director of Vacation Bible School and was thrilled to be working with Christian people helping others, in a small way, to come to know Jesus Christ as their personal Savior. But the dark cloud of divorce hovered over my head like a black sign reading "hypocrite." I had to resign.

At the parsonage, our pastor sat in his recliner, sandwich in one hand and glass of iced sweet tea in the other. I told him, through hiccupping sobs, about the divorce and my faithful assurance that God had greater plans for me and my children. (It had to be through faith since I didn't have much else to get my children and me by.) He stared ahead, not at me—thank goodness! I finished. He took a bite of sandwich and chewed and chewed. It seemed like an eternity. He turned to me. "Do you believe the Lord's forgiven you for the divorce?" I nodded. "Then I don't know why anyone else won't forgive you. Keep the job."

We had a bang-up Bible School!

The process of divorce was long and devastating, even with God's guidance. Accusations, threats, disappointment. But at last, it was "over."

For four hard years I was a single mom. I managed, with God's far-reaching help, to keep bills paid and provide stability and spiritual support for my daughter and son. Divorce freed them from their emotional fears as we experienced God's protection and blessings through His plan for us.

Today, I'm a happy wife of thirty-eight years, mother of two successful and happily married children (who maintain a relationship with their dad), grandmother of seven, retired teacher, and active church member. I tell others God can do anything—even use divorce for good.

All because I stepped out in faith.

* * *

Cheryl Gore Pollard graduated from the University of West Georgia where she earned three teaching degrees, Gifted

Certification, and National Board Certification. She retired in 2010. Cheryl is the author of seven books, all published and available on Amazon. Cheryl believes that "to be a mentor and support to any divorcee is a gift from God."

31

THE RIVER OF LIFE

BY RICHELLE HATTON

I followed the winding, dirt path through the fragrant bush until it ended abruptly at a trickling creek. A large, flat rock completely blocked the path of the water. In fact, the only way for the water to continue its journey was to fall down a hole in the rock, into the darkness below.

I heard God whisper, "So it will be with you. The water is your life, and a time is coming when the only way forward will be to go down into darkness. You won't see where you're going. There are obstacles to negotiate, but do not be afraid! I will be with you, and I will help you find your way."

As I looked further downstream, I noticed that eventually the water flowed out from underneath the rock and into a peaceful pool. "The darkness will not last forever," God promised. "The suffering and hardship will end, and I will bring you to a place of rest and peace." What could it mean?

* * *

For weeks I had been having puzzled conversations with Stephen's parents. He would tell us odd things God was saying to him. They sounded almost right but not quite. We couldn't put our finger on the problem. We watched and waited for clarity.

It finally came over a period of twenty-four hours that changed everything. Stephen and I stayed up all night. He believed God was sending a truck full of items and it would arrive at any time. We had to be ready! Each time it didn't arrive when he had predicted, Stephen just changed his story.

He was so sure, even though it made absolutely no sense. In the morning, his story changed again, and it became clear something was dreadfully wrong.

I needed help. I had no idea what to do so I phoned my mother-in-law. She came and called the mental health team. My father-in-law came and hid all the knives. I was horrified—was that really necessary? We waited, all day, for help to arrive. The mental health team finally came at 9:00 PM. Stephen was completely unresponsive—catatonic—unable to talk or even acknowledge anyone. He told me later he believed if he spoke, we would all die a horrible death by fire. Can you imagine? He was so terrified that his mind and body shut down in response to his terrifying delusions.

Stephen was hospitalized the next day, in the psychiatric ward. It was a surreal place, a refuge from reality. I didn't tell our friends the whole truth of where he was. Stephen responded well to treatment and was soon sent home. I felt lost. I had no road map for dealing with mental illness and recovery.

God, however, knew this would happen. He had warned me, prepared me, and he was still with me. Especially now, when I felt all alone and out of my depth. His warning gave me comfort.

Nothing was a mystery to him. Knowing this difficult situation would not last forever helped me to press on.

We negotiated the unfamiliar roads of mental illness and recovery together, and our marriage was strengthened as a result. Stephen tells his story now, about his battle with mental illness. It is no longer a terrible secret we must hide. Secrets have power over you. But we have found that speaking the truth out loud releases the grip on our hearts and minds imposed by secrecy. As Jesus taught, the truth sets us free.

Sharing the truth has also brought us friends who have supported us through a relapse, even to the point of visiting Stephen in the psychiatric ward. Unthinkable the first time around, it was so healing to face the monster within the caring embrace of friendship rather than on my own. Of course, I was never really alone at all. As He promised that day by the creek, and also in His word, Jesus is always with me.

Recently, I went back to that creek, and this time, God led me to the other end, where it joined with the river. He showed me that my life has moved forward and is now mingled with the river, with His family of faith. It's time to share what I've learned, so that others may benefit. God loves deeply. His certain, constant presence brings comfort throughout the journey of life. He goes before us and prepares the way. He walks beside us through both joys and sorrows. He leads and guides His people and sets us free to follow him. God is good and all is well.

***

Richelle Hatton can usually be found reading well into the night. Otherwise, you may find her in her classroom, teaching and inspiring ten-year-olds, or preparing exciting lessons. Stephen, her beloved husband of thirty years and her biggest supporter, will be close by, probably with cookies and a cup of tea.

32

LIVING WITH A ONE-ARMED MAN

BY TERRIE TODD, 3RD PLACE WINNER

*W*hat do you do when you discover you've become the proverbial "other people" to whom certain things happen?

In May of 1995, a job lay-off caused my husband, Jon, to take work on a potato farm to tide us over until something more permanent came along. He enjoyed the work and the people, and Autumn found them fully into the swing of harvest.

On September 29, our lives changed forever. While attempting to brush dirt away from the belt of a live-bottom trailer, Jon's right arm became caught between belt and roller, trapping him for what seemed forever until a fellow worker reached him and shut the truck off. Several men were required to free him from the machinery. By the end of the day, Jon found himself settled into a hospital bed, clods of black field dirt still in his hair, and his right arm amputated five inches above the elbow.

I returned home and gave the news to our three kids. Two days later marked our eighteenth wedding anniversary, and I fell asleep that night with the words of our marriage vows flowing through my mind. *For better, for worse, in sickness and in health, till death do us part.* How thankful I felt that death hadn't parted us yet, and that God had equipped Jon for this challenge by giving him an incredibly patient, determined, and resourceful spirit.

After such a loss, you're dealing with a lot at once. If you think you can't imagine it, try this: tie your dominant hand behind your back and leave it there. Now shower, dress, and fix your hair. Butter your toast, open a carton of milk, and peel yourself an orange. Don't forget to take the medication they put in a child-proof container for you. Now tie your boots and zip your coat. Run some errands. Sign some checks. Try to understand that tomorrow you must do it all over again ... and the day after that ... and the day after that.

On the upside, imagine dozens of cards, fruit baskets, baking, groceries, and meals showing up at your door. Imagine your church family collecting money for you and helping with farm work and snow-blowing. Know that hundreds of prayers are going up for you, and feel their power as God sustains you and gives you grace to thank Him for sparing your life. Know He has a plan in this, that it did not surprise Him. Observe as others feel blessed and drawn closer to God because of it all. Enjoy the closeness among family that comes with facing trials together. Know you are loved and cared for by more people than you ever realized. Experience in a new way the peace of God, which surpasses all understanding as it guards your heart and mind. Allow God to comfort you through Scriptures like Isaiah 41:10: "Do not fear, for I am with you; do not be dismayed, for I am your God. I will strengthen you and help you; I will uphold you with my righteous right hand."

Someone asked me recently how this event changed our lives—or more specifically, how it changed mine. Though our lives have been forever divided into "before and after," here's a little of what I've learned.

1) I've learned that one can question God and survive. What

do you do with a faith that knows God can heal but asks why He does not? Although I no longer feel angry when I hear of others receiving healing, I still don't understand. What I do know is that God has not struck me dead for such faithless thoughts.

2) I've learned to be a little more considerate. I'll change the toilet paper roll before it runs out so Jon won't need to. I leave the twist-tie off the bread bag, place all his silverware on the left side of his plate, and trim his fingernails.

3) I've learned gratitude. Gratitude for having a husband who is still alive, who can walk and talk and think—and who loves me, stays with me, and does his best to support his family when many able-bodied men do not. Gratitude for God's faithfulness in providing our needs. Gratitude for children who learned much about integrity and faithfulness because this happened to their father.

4) I have learned to anticipate Heaven even more. There, all of us will enjoy perfect, healthy, beautiful bodies that will never grow weary, minds that will never think selfish or evil thoughts, souls that will worship God in holy purity forever.

Through the tears, anger, and frustration, God made Himself real to us. Whatever the future holds, we know Who holds the future. He is our Peace, our Hope, our Rock, our Jesus.

* * *

Terrie Todd is a faith and humor columnist, playwright, author of historical novels, blogger at www.terrietodd.blogspot.com, and winner of six Word Guild Awards and the Inscribe Christian Writers Fellowship 2018 Janette Oke Award. Terrie lives with her husband, Jon, in Manitoba, Canada, where they raised their three children.

33

LOVING AN ADDICT

BY STEPHANIE LOGAN

A table would be pretty useless without legs. The tabletop is the piece that everyone looks at. We buy decorative pieces that are beautiful, but no one thinks much about the legs that support the table. This is where we gather with friends and family to laugh, share, and make memories. And no one even seems aware of the burden borne by the supporting legs. Time out.

Why are we talking about tables?! Here is a chapter from the story of the burden of addiction.

This is what it's like when you love an addict. This is the mostly unseen burden of addiction. Most of us loved ones are the support. All eyes are on the one with the drug problem, and those of us closest to the addict aren't seen much. We stay behind the scenes, desperately grasping for any possible tool that provides even a glimmer of hope that something might work, something might help. Our loved ones? They don't know what to say. It's just too much. The problem is too big. The pain is too extreme. And we, the loved ones of the addict? We don't know what to say either.

Many of us have lived our whole lives in the background,

quietly watching and observing, always aware of our surroundings and looking to see how we fit into the grand scheme of things. So, when we are dealing with the consequences of the active substance abuse of the one we love so deeply, we revert to the place that we're most comfortable. Behind the scenes, quietly watching in the background. This is the place where we carry the burden of addiction in silence. That's not to say we're not trying to take action. But those of us who have been down this road have learned well that there's really very little we can do. Often times, the best we can do is pray.

So pray, I did. Night after night I settled my children into bed and found myself a quiet place to pray and cry. For two years, this was my routine. I prayed that my husband would change—that I would change. I prayed for strength, wisdom, patience, and anything else I could grasp at. And I cried. Most nights I cried until I finally drifted to sleep.

You see, I knew what was coming if something didn't change fast. And my husband? He couldn't hear me pointing out that something was wrong. He seemed to have closed his ears to any such feedback. After beating my head against the proverbial wall trying to get the message across for several months, I stopped. I stopped talking to him about what was bothering me. I can't pinpoint the day this change occurred. I don't think it happened in one day. It happened over a span of time. I can tell you this, though: Our relationship has never been the same since that day. I didn't love him less. I wasn't angry, necessarily. It's more like I just became aware he wasn't going to hear me, and the best thing I could do was focus on the things that I could control. He and his choices and actions weren't among those things.

I didn't become less sad after that day. It's just that I chose not to fight anymore. And I prayed even more fervently. I read everything I could get my hands on pertaining to our situation,

TRIUMPH FROM TRAGEDY

and I allowed myself time to cry. Looking back on it, I can see that I was grieving a loss I knew was coming long before the loss actually occurred. So, when the day came, I was already well into the grieving process. This is a chapter from the untold story of the burden of addiction.

Over the course of my husband's relapse, I noticed that, in the early days, anyone who was aware of what had really been going on in our lives scattered. People were uncertain how they should engage with us, and no one likes to be uncertain. As time went on and on, I finally became able to speak openly about my experience with those who really loved me. I made new friends very slowly, and two years later, when we began to piece our lives back together, we began adding new friends to our circle. I began to notice that people seem to love a good underdog story. Everyone loves to hear stories like this one.

My husband's story, in a nutshell, sounds something like this: "I had been clean for several years and then I relapsed. My wife and kids left, and I went on a downward spiral. I ultimately reached a point where I could no longer take the torture of active addiction, and I began to make some different choices and do the hard work of recovery. Now, my wife and I are back together, the kids are thriving, and we still have work to do, but we are doing very well."

This is part of his own story of the burden of addiction. Doesn't that sound like a great story?! Very inspiring. People eat it up. My story is different.

My story would tell of the boring details of doing life.

I went to work every day. I raised my children and learned how to do life as a single mom. I paid the bills. I searched for healing. I learned to embrace the pain, and then let it go. And today, I'm still healing, but I am doing much better.

My story is more about what you don't hear. The nutshell version of my story doesn't have time to tell you that I went to work every day in agonizing pain. Or that everything I did seemed utterly empty without being able to share it with the person I had meant to share my life with. It doesn't have time to tell you of the bravery it took for me to finally open up and talk about it, or the painstaking effort it took to find the answers to the questions my children were asking. It won't tell you of the paralyzing fear I would not be able to provide for my family. There are a lot of things it won't tell you. So, when I tell you mine, it won't seem inspiring. But it is.

It is because I did some things wrong along the way, but there was so much that I did right.

The point? All eyes are still on the tabletop. Most people still aren't aware of the burden borne by the supporting legs. In the beginning, all eyes were on the one with the drug problem. Now, all eyes are on the one who overcame it. And most people have no idea that those of us who were part of the whole story very nearly cracked under the pressure. Both stories—my husband's and mine—are true and accurate. But they're not the whole story. Each is only a snapshot.

I wrote this piece because I know. I know it gets lonely. I know we sometimes feel discredited. I know we do a lot that no one will likely ever know about. I know we get tired sometimes of feeling like we are living in the shadow of another. I know we don't talk about it because when we do it doesn't sound pretty.

If I'm being honest, even now I'm struggling with the words I'm writing. Why? Because it's not about who gets the attention. Trust me, I don't want it. It's about knowing that the difficult work that I did—the difficult work that we do—has value. It makes a difference. It's worth something. It's worth a lot, actually. And while we choose not to be the focal point, our role is still important. I know this. But it took me a long time to learn it. And now I'm telling you. Your story has value. The details that no one knows about are likely the ones that make the biggest difference. Your pain and healing, your efforts and your contribution, it all matters, and you need to know it.

***

Stephanie Logan knows that helpers wear a lot of hats. By day, she is a full-time counselor, a wife, and a mom of three. She is a musician, a writer, a daughter, and a sister. But in all of the roles she plays, there are always undertones of the helper in her. She hopes her writing will help you in some way. So, grab your coffee, relax, and read on.

34

GOODBYE MOUNTAIN

BY FRANCES KING ABRAMS

*A*s my husband, Jerome, lay beside me in the rented beach condo, his breathing seemed in sync with the distant ebb and flow of the surf. He had completed six weeks of radiation treatments after being diagnosed with glioblastoma multiforme, a lethal brain tumor. I had assumed that if I could only get Jerome to his favorite beach spot, he would feel better after the treatments. But he didn't. He was exhausted.

Doctors had informed us of the grim prognosis of GBM, nicknamed "The Beast," but we refused to give in to it. A year earlier, Jerome had begun a new ministry as a local area director of missions after decades as a pastor and church staff member. At age sixty, he still had ministry to give and poured himself into the new role as an opportunity to encourage the ministers in his care.

Listening to the waves and Jerome's breaths, I prayed, "Lord, You told Your disciples that if they had faith in God, they could say to a mountain, 'Be taken up and cast into the sea,' and if they believed, it would happen" (Mark 11:23-24). "Lord, I believe You can take this brain tumor away from Jerome." I imagined a large fish swimming away with the brain tumor after God cast it into the Gulf of Mexico.

Our beach trip was disastrous. Jerome was too tired to enjoy a vacation and sometimes became confused. Yet, with hundreds of prayer warriors standing with us, we trusted that Jerome would be healed against the odds. Without treatment, the maximum life expectancy was three months. We opted for treatments to slow the tumor's growth. We had hopeful moments when chemotherapy diminished the cancer. Then it would return with vengeance, each time robbing my husband of a cherished ability. I watched Jerome deteriorate before my eyes. The mountain was not moving.

Each visit from our children and grandchildren revealed the stark reality that Jerome was slipping away from them. As the disease progressed, Jerome forgot our children's names and began to treat the grandchildren as strangers. He later forgot my name.

An early symptom of his illness was confused speech. As the disease progressed, he could neither understand the words he read nor speak the words he meant. This was frustrating for a man who had loved reading and studying, had earned graduate degrees, and whom God had called to preach.

One day, a group of ministers came to lay their hands on Jerome and pray for his healing. As they started to leave, they asked to voice a final prayer. To their astonishment, before they began Jerome voiced an almost flawless prayer.

On another occasion, when Jerome's eyes were closed, I asked if he were asleep. He shook his head. "Are you praying?" I asked.

"Yes!"

"You are growing very close to God lately, aren't you?"

Another emphatic "Yes!"

As the tumor pressed on his brain stem and hospice care was advised, I came to accept that the "small miracles" our family had seen—Jerome's ability to voice prayers when he couldn't converse, the closeness to God that he communicated, the provision of our financial needs, the support of friends—were preparation for the greatest miracle of all: Jerome's entrance into the presence of Christ.

In the early morning of February 22, 2009, Jerome's hyperventilating awakened me. Later, his breathing slowed like the ebb and flow of the waves during our beach trip. As I held his hand in the stillness, he took his final breath and was ushered into Heaven.

On that early Sunday morning, I recall that I kept repeating through my tears, "My Precious, my Precious, my Precious." During Jerome's memorial service, a minister quoted Psalm 116:15: "Precious in the sight of the Lord is the death of His Godly ones" (NASB).

I had asked God to remove Jerome's tumor. Instead, He allowed us to say "Goodbye" to a mountain of pain, frustration, and fear when Jerome said "Goodbye" to this sinful world and "Hello" to his eternal home.

From these memories I have confirmed what I know of God's nature: God is all-knowing and wise. He knows the future that we cannot see. We who trust in Christ are assured of ultimate healing when our mortal bodies die. That healing is eternal life with Him.

God is the sovereign ruler of the universe. He is God, and we are not. We should pray earnestly for our wants and needs, remembering that He answers in alignment with His perfect will.

"For now we see in a mirror dimly, but then face to face; now I know in part, but then I will know fully just as I also have been fully known" (1 Corinthians 13:12 NASB).

* * *

Frances King Abrams is writing her first book, *The Widow's Song*, a collection of devotions for widows. She has been a freelance magazine writer and a newspaper staff writer and *Lifestyles* editor. She was the public information writer for Chambers County (Alabama) Board of Education from 1998-2010 before her retirement.

35

WILL SOMEONE PLEASE TELL ME WHEN TO BREATHE?

BY KATHY STEPHENS

The vacuum sound of the emergency room doors led to the pounding of feet. It was like a stampede of wild horses vibrating the floor. Five men were running with my husband on a gurney. A blurred vision remains of that moment with him in a full-blown code. Breathe.

I stepped out of the waiting room.

My mind's eye was watching intently their every move, but my insides were screaming, "Can't you see that he is dead?" Breathe....

I was forced back into the waiting room. *Tick tock, tick tock* said the clock on the wall. I remember burying my face in my hands. I had taken myself into my hiding place, and I had begun rocking back and forth so as to soothe my soul. After what seemed like an eternity, I could see three sets of feet appear through the cracks of my fingers that covered my face. I could hear them calling my name but I thought, *If I don't look up, then they can't tell me anything.*

The words I heard next were deafening. "Mrs. Stephens, we are so sorry, but there was nothing we could do." Breathe....

Everything I knew about life died in that moment. Dennis

was the love of my life for twenty-three years. He became my game changer after many years of emotional events. The heartbreak of divorce, the loss of my father at an early age, and my mother moving us away from everything I'd ever known, were damaging. Dennis taught me so much about true love and absolute trust on this side of heaven.

That night in the ER became the most pivotal day of my life.

Pivotal means to change course, reset, shift, or re-establish. Pivotal moments come in the middle of loss, disappointment, rejection, bad choices, abuse ... and much more. We grow from pivotal moments. Did you hear that? Read it again. *We grow from pivotal moments.*

Now for the aftermath—the *do or die moment.*

Weeks after Dennis's death, I found myself numb and prayer was unattainable. I found myself in a valley of despair. I was hopeless and confused. Late one Sunday afternoon, as I sat alone crying, I found myself face down in our bed. I pulled his pillow close to my chest, and what began as an uncontrollable sob turned into a desperate cry for help. "God please help me. I can't breathe." I spent hours that afternoon with a pouring out of all that I was. I experienced moans and groans from such deep pain.

Then it happened ... God met me in that place. His presence was indescribable. The Holy Spirit began speaking softly to me. He spoke about letting go of trying to control my pain, my anguish, and to stop trying to figure it all out. He whispered, *"Simply depend on the One who knows your every need."* On that day, God took something broken and began to mold it into something beautiful.

If you have your life all planned out and you think you are in charge of everything, just hold on, because a pivotal moment is coming.

The tapestry in our lives is woven by the pivotal moments we survive; however, you have to believe you *can* and *will* survive. Survival doesn't look the same for everyone. You are forever changed inside a pivotal moment.

God isn't surprised by anything we endure. He is right there waiting on us to lean into Him, to totally surrender. He is watching for us to raise our white flag.

My worst nightmare has become my greatest walk with God. God has revealed Himself to me in new ways, and He has proven that He is able in all things.

If you find yourself in waters that seem too deep, back out and let God go in first. He uses everything in our lives to reveal Himself to us.

Your story isn't over, and my story isn't over. God still has a purpose and a plan for each of our lives.

What you know about Christ matters, but who you are *in* Christ matters more.

Over time, God has held me, whispered to me, and has allowed me to see just how short life really is. Grief is strong enough to change us, but God is powerful enough to make that change for good. Make it count and remember to breathe.

He heals the brokenhearted and bandages their wounds (Psalms 147:3).

* * *

Kathy Stephens is a wellness advocate, certified Christian Yoga Instructor, Christian life coach, and a graduate in Women's Ministry from the New Orleans Baptist Theological Seminary. She has been published in *Christian Yoga Magazine*.

36

LOOKING THROUGH THE ETHER OF THINGS

BY ANN-ELIZABETH BLAIR WATT

*L*ike everyone, we've had our fair share of catastrophic weather conditions before. But this time an unhappy whirlwind would transport us out into the murky ether. Tragedy would not pass us by, but rather would have its way with us. Still reeling, my feet are struggling to land on solid ground.

First big thing, my husband and I would move in with our daughter (who lives five minutes away), their two young children aged seven and ten, and her husband, who was battling what would prove to be an extremely aggressive form of Stage 4, T-cell lymphoma. Paul was our most outstanding son-in-law, the sort of man every mother's wildest dreams tempt her to believe her daughter might have the fortuitousness to marry. He would be undergoing many rounds of the strongest chemotherapies created by mankind, and two complete bone marrow transplants. He would be happily declared in remission during the year 2020.

Desiring to help them, we moved into their beautiful country home and acreage with about one-third of our furniture. My baby grand piano landed in their living room, as I can't live without it. They didn't seem to mind the overflow. For our part, we were determined not to consider any of this a sacrifice.

Sadly, all did not turn out as I hoped for, or even as expected, and we are back in our own home now. Our beloved daughter is a very young widow. My heart has shattered into a million pieces as her delightful children have lost a most highly involved, even doting, father. Neither experience, that of the widow or the "orphans" before such tremendous loss, can ever be replaced. The sense of permanence, of finality, is profound.

The year 2021 has not been good to us. Our dear Paul, the son I loved as one of my own, was cruelly taken from us. He died on May 13 of this year.

And through the ether, I have prayed.

As an anesthetic, ether is an agent that dulls one's senses and makes reality fade away. As a child having my tonsils removed, I remember a sweetly pungent, moistened cloth placed over my nose and mouth. I was told to count backwards from ten, making it almost to eight. I tried to say it, but the word wouldn't come out. And, oh, how dizzying of the room, which would then become a rocket ride to Outer Space (I've always had an active imagination).

Back to the present. When I sleep now, it's fitfully. And when I awaken, all is well for a few graciously dulled moments of time, and then I remember.

Praying has helped. God knows. I tell Him all about it regularly, with a commitment that borders on obsession. Sometimes I ask His Holy Spirit to intercede for me when those words don't come out right.

Sharing my pain with caring friends has been perhaps the best balm to my soul. I've been overcome with sweet tears of relief by their loving acts of kindness.

The dragon of grief takes a long time with a person. Grabs one by the neck, shakes him around ever-so-violently 'til nearly a stupor replaces his consciousness. When its victim finally reawakens, unavoidable damage to the heart and mind having occurred and the world appears "different." Even colors have changed. The hospital-green of walls we remember so well, will swirl throughout an otherwise gray fog. Edges will blur, caused by tears or stress.

I call it, "looking through the ether of things."

It's this way for me now. I'm smack dab in the middle of grief's passageways, a labyrinth with no straightforward way out.

So, I sit or lie down when reality overwhelms—dwell with it, this swirling assault upon my exquisite sensibilities. Nothing makes much sense at all now. Be advised by the pain (better yet, invite God to speak to my wounded soul, to come alongside right within this cruel fog), and only get up and move on when the level of attack feels like, "Together, God and I can do this." Then, arise to take on the next moment in time. When I am simply "whelmed," then it's time for one-foot-before-the-other again.

The next big thing will be regaining my life purpose, now. Triumph? It's not happened yet, but I believe it will come.

I don't understand God's purposes in visiting such terrible tragedy upon our most precious daughter and her tender, impressionable children.

Meanwhile, we visit ice cream parlors in the summertime.

* * *

Ann-Elizabeth Blair Watt (B.A) is a pianist, author, and illustrator of a children's book who loves flowers, baking, and interior design. She is a pastor's wife, a Bible study teacher, staff supporter, event planner, and a camp counselor instructing art and tennis.

37

NOT. THAT. STORY

BY GAYLE CHILDRESS GREENE

I am a writer. I wanted my life to be a story. A heartwarming, documentary-worthy story like rescuing an abandoned gosling. Under my care, the clumsy baby bird would grow into a beautiful goose and fly away. It would return to my front porch every year at the same time to say hello. Now *that's* a story.

But my life was happily normal and predictable. No babies showing up on the doorstep. No long-lost identical twin sister. No abandoned gosling. Nothing unusual or out of the ordinary. A husband, two dogs, and three grown children who were leaving our nest one-by-one. Like my imaginary goose, I let go of them, hoping they would always be able to find our front porch.

One day, the earth shifted beneath my feet, and a story came. It was not the script I wanted to be written. Not the story of my twenty-six-year-old daughter being diagnosed with multiple sclerosis. Not the story of my first grandchild being born with a rare condition called arthrogryposis multiplex congenita, a disease affecting his arms.

Not. That. Story.

What would my daughter's future hold? How would my grandson brush his teeth or scratch his nose? I tried to have faith, to believe in God's goodness, but I was overwhelmed by fear. I was a mother. I was a fixer. But I couldn't fix this. I could not make it all better with a band-aid and a kiss. It was too big for me. The firm foundation that had held me since I was a little girl turned to quicksand, and I began to sink.

"Trust me, my child." I heard the familiar voice of my Savior. "I am the Author. You are the page."

They say you shouldn't struggle if you step into a pool of quicksand or you'll go down faster. But I panicked. I scratched and clawed, trying to escape the story.

"Please, God, please ... give me the MS. Let me have the disability. Let me take the burden from them," I begged the Lord.

"No, my daughter," He calmly replied, and I went under. The earth engulfed and choked me. I was lost. There was no air. There was no gosling.

When you pass through the waters, I will be with you (Isaiah 43:2).

Suddenly, His strong arms wrapped around my waist. But instead of taking me toward the light, I was pulled down. Down through the tears, down through the doubt, down through the "whys." During my descent, His strong arms never let go of me. But He was not going to rescue me. He was going to take me through the pain.

So do not fear, for I am with you. Don't be discouraged, for I am your God. I will strengthen you and help you. I will uphold you with my victorious right hand (Isaiah 41:10).

I don't know how long my crisis of faith lasted, but it wasn't days or weeks or months. It was years. Finally, one day I was ready to accept the story the Lord was writing.

If we are faithless, He will remain faithful, for He cannot disown Himself (2 Timothy 2:13).

"Do you love Me, my child?" My Savior asked gently in the darkness.

"Yes, Lord, I love You."

"Do you trust Me?"

"I trust You."

"Even if I never heal your daughter or your grandson?"

"Even if You never heal them."

Then something happened, a ray of hope warmed my heart. Small seeds of faith and trust began to take root and grow. Like those fragile seedlings, I emerged through the soil of circumstances that had tried to crush my faith.

"You have learned one of life's most difficult lessons." The Lord smiled and wiped the dirt and tears from my face. "Now, let's continue your amazing story. Fix your eyes on Me. I am the Author and Perfecter of your faith, and I promise you'll love the ending."

Hope in God, for I shall again praise Him (Psalm 43:5).

* * *

Gayle Childress Greene is a children's book author, award-winning playwright, and sporadic blogger. Her most recent writing endeavor, *Because You Are Mine,* was illustrated by her daughter and published by Climbing Angel Publishing.

EXTRA BLESSINGS

BY KARLA DEE

I was diagnosed with breast cancer in 2008, and I chose to have a double mastectomy. That October, while in my final stages of reconstruction, my husband of twenty years wrote me a letter that said, "You have been a good wife, but I have found someone else. I want a divorce."

With help, I found a home my two girls and I could afford and feel safe in. But within only three months of moving in, we received an eviction notice. The house we were renting was already in foreclosure. Praises to God for providing the next home we lived in for the next twenty months.

Poor financial decisions during my marriage, and the lack of a second income, eventually forced me to file for bankruptcy. During these days, I clung to God for survival. For the first time in my life, I began reading the Bible daily.

The next year, my older daughter graduated high school and left for college. That caused the child support from my ex-husband to decrease. My younger daughter wanted to be in the same high school as her church friends, and I knew we needed to downsize and move into her desired school district.

I scoured the Internet for a rental home but had no luck.

Due to my bankruptcy, it should not have been possible for me to buy, but some church friends encouraged me to try. Though I doubted, they pointed out that "with God, all things are possible."

To my astonishment, a bank approved a small loan. It was enough for God to make it work. My friends just smiled, knowing God was working on my behalf. In mid-July, while I was riding the emotional roller coaster of finding a house, my landlord called and told me she had a renter moving in on August 1. I tried not to panic but wondered where we would go.

With no time to spare, we found a house to buy, but I was soon told the house failed to pass inspection.

"Lord," I asked, "what do I do? Do I start searching again? Do I go into a house that is not guaranteed to be mine and try to make the needed improvements?"

About that time, a local missionary family, the Allens, moved into our area. Both of their parents lived in Michigan, so when their son was born, we provided dinner for them. At both Thanksgiving and Easter, I invited them for a gathering. They had lived in their home for a couple of months when they needed to move. Knowing how that felt, I jumped in.

I prayed and felt a peace and a nudge to call the Allens, whom I had known less than a year. I remembered they had an extra room in their home and hoped they might let us live in the extra room for about a month until we could secure an inspection and close on our house.

Before I could ask her, Jenni began to cry. "Karla," she said, "I've had a miscarriage."

I wasn't sure of the exact words to say to her, so I shared words I'd used when I talked about death with a loved one. We talked and talked. My heart was so heavy for her, and I wished her mom had been living near enough to comfort her. In desperation and humility, I eventually turned the conversation toward my initial reason for calling her.

"Jenni," I said, my voice shaking, "I remember your house has an extra bedroom and bath. My daughter and I need a place to live for a month."

Looking back, the only way I think I could have found the words to ask that question came from the Holy Spirit. Perhaps the only reason they were accepted is because they felt it was God's will.

My sixteen-year-old daughter and I became roommates. We worked on the house we were hoping to purchase, praying it would pass inspection and become ours. One month turned into three months. The five of us endured a stomach virus, ate dinners together, and shared household chores. Since Jenni could not pick up anything weighing over five pounds for six weeks, I was able to pick up their son, pick up groceries, and pick up the dishes.

During our short stay (one that seemed very long for all five of us!), we bonded. God not only allowed our house to close, but He gave us some wonderful friends who have since become family. "Nana Karla" are some of the sweetest words ever spoken to me.

Sometimes in life, we find ourselves in undesired situations that are out of our control. Often these issues take us by surprise, but they never take God by surprise. If we trust Him, He will guide us through the problem, filling our cup and allowing it to run over with extra blessings, too.

* * *

Karla Dee is blessed with two grown girls. She has taught school for twenty-nine years. As she nears retirement, she hopes to write more. At age fifty-four, she can say that life is good, not because it is always easy, but because she has God, family, and blessings beyond measure.

39

MY BREAST CANCER JOURNEY

BY JEANETTE BOTHA

October 2019 started with a bang! I felt like I was drowning. I couldn't muster the courage or strength to rise above the waves coming at me with such force and speed that they suffocated me. But let me retract my steps and take you back to September 2019.

I felt a lump in my left breast. I wasn't apprehensive about it. However, the nagging feeling wouldn't leave me, so I phoned the breast clinic and saw them the next day, October first. Not for a moment did I even suspect that something serious could be wrong.

I went for the mammogram and then a sonar. The doctor told me I had cancer in my right breast. She showed me that it was a massive part of my breast. I was overwhelmed, unsure if I should fall into a heap and cry or pull out all the stops and go to war.

After that, I saw the specialist. He confirmed with tests that I had breast cancer, and they needed to remove the mass as soon as possible. All this time, I was praying in the Spirit, declaring the Word over every cancer cell and trying to get to grips with it. Two weeks later, they operated and did a lumpectomy, removing partial breast tissue. At the end of October, I saw the specialist again for my follow up.

I was so full of hope, and I knew the Lord was with me. The doctor told me they couldn't get all the cancer, and that my only option was a total mastectomy of the right breast. According to the tests, I had aggressive breast cancer. Already in my lymphatic system, the procedure needed to be done urgently. The longer I waited, the shorter my chances of survival.

I felt so alone, and my only hope was holding onto the hem of His garment. At times, it felt like I was going to drown. I stood upon the Word, proclaiming it day and night. All I did was pray all the time. I felt the presence of the Lord so firmly over my life.

Many people were praying with me. Finally, as I had no medical coverage, I was referred to the state hospital in Pretoria, South Africa. The Lord was with me, and the way before me was opened miraculously. I could see the head of oncology within the next few days. The treatment plan was the same.

An immediate and aggressive mastectomy. I had to wait for a bed to open up. The list was so long for breast cancer patients. Finally, on the fifteenth of December, I booked into hospital. I was due to be going to the theatre the following day. They postponed my operation to the twenty-third of December. I couldn't go home and had no idea what the Lord was doing, but I knew He had a plan.

All the time, I prayed, proclaimed the Word over myself, and waited on Him. I knew He was in control. Those ten days gave me so much time to sit with the Word, prepare my heart and mind, and just come into His presence. Now looking back, I see so strongly His hand in that time of isolation. It prepared me mentally and emotionally for the road ahead, and physically I could rest. The morning of the twenty-third, I went to the surgical theatre and had a complete and aggressive mastectomy of the right breast.

I have recovered fully now and am completely free of cancer. I see how the Lord was with me all the way. He opened the way to get the right help at the right time. If I had not listened to Him, I would not have made it through this difficult time. Yes, I lost my breast and my lymph nodes in the right arm, but I am alive. I've learned that cancer is not my fault or the consequence of my sin. Bad things do happen to good people, and if they do, we can survive it by the grace of God!

I want to encourage you today: Breast cancer is not the end. Get help as soon as possible. *It's not a shame to get breast cancer. You did nothing wrong.* The statistics worldwide are staggering. Women get breast cancer across ethnicities and different age groups.

- Do regular examinations of your breasts.
- Take the Word and proclaim it over yourself.
- Fall into the loving arms of the Lord Jesus when everything gets to be too much.
- Allow Him to be your comforter and help in times of need.
- Don't go through this alone; get others to pray with you and hold up your arms.

* * *

Jeanette Botha lives in Germiston, South Africa. With a track record of full-time ministry, training up the fivefold ministries for twenty-odd years, counselling practice and international travel, training, and public speaking, she is a living example of God's grace. She is also the author of multiple books and courses.

40

FACING CANCER WITH FAITH

BY KAREN O. ALLEN

*E*very cancer survivor knows it: the day of their diagnosis. For me, it was Friday, January 31, 2003. I felt an enlarged lymph node in my armpit months earlier, but when I had gone to the doctor before to have it checked, it turned out to be nothing. Why should this be any different? I dismissed the warning until I felt it again. This time it was three times larger. The small lump in my breast remained hidden, but praise God, He enabled me to find the enlarged lymph node under my arm.

Biopsy results came back positive. I had hoped statistics would be in my favor, and I would not be the "one" of the one in eight women diagnosed with breast cancer in the U.S. every year. However, I didn't feel that way. I shared my feelings with my husband before going to meet with the surgeon. He assured me that he loved my inner beauty and not just my outward appearance. His words gave me strength to face uncertainties that lay ahead.

Ironically, I worked in a cancer research lab directed by an oncologist. He offered medical leave, but I refused saying that would be the worst thing I could do. I wanted to maintain as normal a schedule as I could at work, at church, and at home.

Surgery came first. Because the lymph node was malignant, as was the tumor in my breast, I would need to undergo chemotherapy. This was devastating news to me. My cancer appeared to be more aggressive than anticipated. I knew I would have to endure seven weeks of radiation therapy, but not an additional five months of chemotherapy.

I adopted the mentality of needing both an effective medical plan (i.e., treatment) and a spiritual plan. My desire to maintain a positive perspective could only come by enhancing my relationship with God through time and intimate communication with Him. Listening and hearing God through meditation, reading Scripture for encouragement and enlightenment, praying for release and direction, shedding tears of sadness and frustration, and looking for signs of His presence kept me centered amid the chaos of the cancer whirlwinds. I leaned upon His promises and found solace in supernatural experiences of reassurance that came through visions, impressions, and symbolism.

An example was my crippling fear of hospitalization. I had never stayed overnight in a hospital and was overwhelmed by the thought. One morning while praying and reading Scripture with soft music playing in the background, I began to weep. All of a sudden, it felt as if Jesus entered my bedroom, walked up to my chair, and asked me to dance. He unleashed my fear by showing me how to let Him lead.

Cancer has the potential for a tragic outcome, but I viewed it as an opportunity—an opportunity to grow my faith. You see, a few months earlier, I prayed to raise my bar of faith. While participating in a book study, I realized I needed to increase my measure of faith to reach beyond myself towards others. Cancer was the chance to demonstrate God's glory in my life. His strength would be the evidence others would see as I traversed this journey of faith.

Truly, the lessons I learned through my suffering continue to this day. First, worship can occur in any place, at any time, including lying under the buzz of a radiation beam or driving a car. Second, praise to our Father offers an element of freedom. I discovered while praising God that I no longer focused on my cancer but upon Him. Needless to say, I found myself praising Him often. Third, having joy in adverse circumstances is possible. When our will is relinquished, and His will is accepted, there is joy. Fourth, faith doesn't always have to feel good. Persecuted Christians know this well. Faith is not based on feeling, but rather on trust followed by obedience. Fifth, a sacrifice of praise gives purpose to suffering. When my hair began falling out, it seemed senseless and defeating. Then I realized I could turn it into a sacrifice of praise. Sixth, contentment is learned and can be rediscovered in time. Seventh, God is in our tomorrows. And eighth ... swallow hard ... glory is often accompanied by suffering.

If I had to pinpoint one takeaway from my experience, it would be that God entered my pain and never, ever left me alone.

As a result of my incredible faith-filled journey, I wrote a Bible study entitled *Confronting Cancer with Faith*. Many have been blessed and encouraged by its inspirational words.

* * *

Karen O. Allen has a passion for music, missions, and writing. Retired from cancer research, she fills her days writing, lunching with friends, and playing the organ. Her Bible study *Confronting Cancer with Faith* (confrontingcancerwithfaith.com) has brought hope around the world. Karen's blog (ewerblessed.com/blog) highlights blessings from life, cancer, and sheep!

41

DRIFTING WITH JESUS

BY MARY SCULLYD

*I*n 2020, when everything was confusing due to the COVID-19 virus, I felt a lump in my breast. Out of the blue, I felt tingling in my fingers. I tried shaking it off, but the tingling lingered. I did not think of going to see a doctor right away. The lines at Urgent Care were extremely long.

Some hospitals were only seeing patients fighting COVID, and other specialists were not even taking new patients.

However, my spiritual mentor persuaded me to see an oncologist as soon as possible. She hears from God, and I trust her explicitly. So, I made the call and was pleasantly surprised that the process was smoother than I had anticipated. God's favor. The first thing the oncologist did was order an MRI of my brain.

After the MRI, I was only able to do a teleconference with the brain specialist. He said to me, "You have Stage 4 breast cancer." He also told me that I had a few tumors on my brain and recommended gamma-knife radiation. When I heard him say those words, I did not panic. I believe it's because I was praising the Lord through songs of praise and worship right before the call came in. I can't fully explain it, but I was in a state of peace as I heard this terrible diagnosis.

I was about to follow up on the procedure when I contracted COVID-19 and had to self-quarantine. Thankfully, my symptoms were mild—fever for a day and fatigue for two weeks. In this time, God gave me clear instructions for my next steps.

On the day of the radiation, we had a blizzard. Snow was piled so high that no one could get their car out, let alone drive anywhere. It was an answer to prayer that I was introduced to someone who had an SUV that could navigate the snow. He was willing to pick me up at 5:00 AM and drive me the hospital. The long day began as the treatment took about twelve hours. They screwed a helmet on my head. Since the helmet looked like a halo, I joked, declaring I was "the angel of the day."

When I went back to see the brain oncologist a couple of weeks later, I admit I was a little nervous. When he said, "All the tumors are shrinking. In fact, two of them have already disappeared," and "The news could not be any better," I wanted to jump up in joy and thankfulness!

Through this challenging time, and especially when I was in the MRI machines and during the radiation treatment itself, I sensed the peace of God. He showed me a vivid vision. In the vision, I was in a boat. Jesus was with me in the boat, and the boat was drifting. Just drifting ….

According to the dictionary, *drifting* means to be carried or moved along smoothly or effortlessly. I sense Jesus was carrying me through this ordeal. I sense total peace as I drifted in the boat with Jesus.

If you are currently facing a health crisis, I urge you to seek God for your healing. There are many healing Scriptures in the Bible, but they will not work until you believe it for yourself. Your faith is also voice-activated. Don't be afraid to confess the promises of God out loud. "For I will restore your health to you and heal you of your wounds, says the Lord" (Jeremiah 30:17).

Then, listen to the Holy Spirit to guide you to your next steps. The solution may be different for each person, but the spirit of life from God is the same. He may tell you to do something practical. Do it. I heard Holy Spirit tell me to eat walnuts. Later, I read walnuts are good for your brain. God speaks; be listening.

Thirdly, refuse to hear anything other than God's Word for your situation. His Word is always about life. Jesus came to give you an abundant life. Do not accept any death reports or negative talk. Believe God's promises and fight for your life!

Remember, you have an enemy who is out to destroy you. But don't forget that God had sent His Son, your Savior Jesus Christ, to destroy the works of the enemy. Learning how to take God at His Word, and speaking out in the authority God has given to you, are keys to your healing.

Believe that God loves you and God wants you well. Don't give up!

"My friend, I am praying that all is well with you and that you enjoy good health in the same way that you prosper spiritually" (3 John 1:2).

* * *

Mary ScullyD is passionate about empowering believers to know their identity in Jesus Christ so that they can experience healing and enjoy a healthy life. Mary has been healed from childhood sexual abuse, emotional rejection, and breast cancer. She is a fierce prayer warrior and exhibits a joy-for-life that overflows to those around her. You can learn more about Mary on her website: www.maryscullyd.com and her Facebook: www.facebook.com/MaryScullyD.

42

BREAKING THROUGH THE LABYRINTH OF MENTAL ILLNESS

BY SHARON ATWOOD

If the truth had been known, I may have never been conceived. Doctors said it wasn't possible. My mother hoped they were right. They were not, and here I am—living proof that mental illness is inheritable. My father's schizophrenia found a new home in me and morphed into bipolar disorder.

Looking back on my life, it is easy to see tragedy take center stage. However, a light shines through the tragic darkness to illuminate a triumphant curtain call.

Mental illness first reared its ugly head during my junior year of high school. A break-up with my boyfriend, plus the pressures of final exams, catapulted me into a nervous breakdown. In junior college, mental illness gurgled up again with new demands and deadlines. Having been a straight-A student in high school, I became suicidal when I made a D on a math test.

By my junior year at Birmingham-Southern College, mental illness closed in like a shroud. My dorm room became an escape to lull my depression to sleep. Mood instability led to my first hospitalization in the psychiatric ward where I was stamped with the label of bipolar disorder. I returned to school but was hospitalized two more times—once when my parents divorced and then again just before graduation.

Bipolar symptoms flare up with extreme stress. When my mother was diagnosed with brain cancer and my father became suicidal, I was overwhelmed and required hospitalization. Unable to fulfill my student teaching for graduate school, I had to forego my teaching certificate.

Mental illness can cause reckless behavior. Three specific instances come to mind. The first was when I went to a hotel for a change of environment to de-stress. While there, I imagined my phone to be filled with derogatory comments pushing me to the brink of jumping off the balcony ledge. The second was when I drove to Georgia seeking help for mania. While at the Atlanta airport, I narrowly escaped being kidnapped into human trafficking. The third instance was another spontaneous effort to find help, this time in Florida. I left without telling anyone. I had no money, no driver's license, and little gas; but I did have my cat! I was gone for six weeks.

Mental illness leaves no facet of life untouched. Employment, social interactions, finances, relationships, decision-making, self-care, even driving are influenced by my bipolar disorder. I've had an above-average number of accidents. The worst was a head-on collision on a one-way street involving a parked police car in front of a police station! I ended up in handcuffs with people surrounding me snapping photos and making videos as I said goodbyes to loved ones.

To help fight against the stigma of mental illness, I have become a representative for the National Alliance on Mental Illness. I travel to various places speaking about my mental health experiences. I am an active member in my church and serve as a volunteer in the community. Currently, I am writing a devotional book geared towards the mental health population and their advocates.

Psychiatric hospitalizations are becoming a distant past. My psychiatrist and psychologist say that I am a success story, having come from severe psychosis to being a functioning member of society. For me, that is cause for celebration.

* * *

Born and raised in rural Alabama, **Sharon Atwood** knows about country living, though now a city girl in Birmingham. Her love for poetry is echoed through her speaking as a representative for the National Alliance on Mental Illness. Her short stories are found in the *Short & Sweet* book series.

43

DON'T ASK WHY, ASK WHAT

ESTHER M. BANDY

I struggled to move my hand, but I couldn't. Mosquitos continued to bite me through the mosquito net. I tried to call out to my husband. If he moved my hand, the mosquitos would stop biting. But he was in another room, and my voice was merely a whisper. I was alone. Then I remembered. The Lord was with me.

"Lord, please help me, or send Jim to help."

A few minutes later, my husband arrived. "Honey, do you need anything?"

I said a silent thank you to God and told Jim about the mosquitos. After he moved my hand, he fixed me tea and held the cup while I drank.

I didn't understand why my strange attacks kept happening. We were missionaries in Mexico, and we'd been doing outdoor evangelistic ministry. But after spending time outside, I'd get sick. I often had headaches and abdominal pain, and sometimes vomiting and weakness. At times, I was too weak to get out of bed or move my body.

"Why, Lord? What's wrong with me? Please heal me."

I gradually improved from that attack, but the intermittent

problems happened more often. I'd had mild attacks before moving to Mexico, but my doctors hadn't found anything wrong with me. In Mexico, the attacks had gotten worse.

I knew God could heal me, so we kept praying. We loved the Mexican people and the ministry God had given us. We longed to stay there and continue serving the Lord.

Still, I looked forward to our next border trip. Every six months we traveled to Texas to renew our visas. While there, we'd visit the churches that prayed for us and supported us financially. If we had health problems, we'd see the doctor. I made plans to find different doctors on our next trip. I hoped they'd find out what was wrong with me. In the meantime, I'd limit my time in the sun.

In Texas, I explained my symptoms to my new doctor, and he ordered numerous tests. On my follow-up visit I was hopeful he'd tell me what was wrong. We listened as he shared the results of my tests and gave me his diagnosis.

"I can't find anything wrong with you. Your problem is in your mind. Live your life and focus on the positive."

Was he right? Were my problems just my imagination? We returned to Mexico, and I was determined to be positive and do whatever we wanted to do without worrying about my health. I was going to stay well.

Unfortunately, I had even more attacks. Some included difficulty breathing, and I was often confined to bed for days. This was not my imagination, so I became even more careful to avoid the sun.

On our next border trip, I saw another doctor. His diagnosis?

"I don't know what's wrong with you, but you need to stay out of the sun. I'm going to write to your mission board and tell them you need to leave Mexico if you want to live."

I was devastated, but my husband and I agreed. Our son was only twelve, and we didn't want him to grow up without a mother. I was also getting too sick to be much help on the mission field. After four years, we were leaving Mexico.

We studied climate charts then moved to Rochester, NY. They needed a CEF director, so we became directors, and we taught Spanish at a Christian school. I still had symptoms and visited more doctors. After ten years of searching for answers, I was finally diagnosed with a type of porphyria that affects the skin and the nervous system. Two years later, I was disabled and mostly homebound. Eventually we had to cover the windows in our home with black plastic to block out the sunlight.

I asked God, "Why is this happening to me?" I longed to serve the Lord, but I was in and out of the hospital and often too sick to get out of bed. I searched the Bible and listened to preachers, hoping for answers.

In a powerful message, David Ring said, "Don't ask *why*, ask *what*."

Instead of asking God why this was happening, I began asking, "Lord, what do you want me to do now?"

I realized that God's plan and purpose for me was more important than my temporary pain. I studied the Bible and memorized Scripture. The Bible blessed me and strengthened me.

Psalm 119:71 says, "It is good for me that I have been afflicted; that I might learn thy statutes."

Eventually, I remembered that as a second grader I wanted to be a nurse, a missionary, a teacher, and a writer. I'd done the first three. Now, it was time to write.

God's plan is perfect.

* * *

Esther M. Bandy received Christ at age five. She says it was "the most important day of my life." She has worked as a nurse, a missionary, and a Spanish teacher. Now she has become a writer, writing her debut picture book and debut middle grade novel.

44

SURRENDER

BY CHRISTEL OWOO

Naturally, I am an independent person and find it extremely difficult to ask for help. One Sunday in March 2019, I walked brightly smiling across a stage during a joyous church anniversary, unaware of what would happen the next day.

The following morning, I bent forward when an excruciating pain hit my lower back. I screamed and tried to move but realized that my back was 'locked-up.' I was in a squat position and tried to get up when another vicious pain shot through my body. I then knew that I had to remain in that posture, so I called my husband for help. I tried to straighten myself before my husband got to me when another pain shoot tormented me, and I realized that I could not sit straight, get up, or move at all. Distressing thoughts ran through my mind; I imagined myself paralyzed for the rest of my life.

My husband called a doctor who diagnosed a muscle strain and said I just needed some rest and I would be fine. Meanwhile, I needed assistance with literally everything, including getting dressed.

Two weeks went by, and I felt another excruciating pain

shoot through my body. An MRI showed that several spine disks in my lower back had cracked and bulged, coupled with damage to my central nervous system. I remained indoors for six months. After some time, I was able to maneuver myself a bit through the house.

The spine injury caused me to halt my leadership role in my church and at work, leaving a vacuum in the church's Ladies Ministry and at the office. At home I had to depend on my husband for simple household chores. And I could not carry my toddler son anymore, affecting the typical mother-child relationship. Eventually, we had to hire a nanny/house helper.

A journey of extreme pain, physical disability, and sedating medication ensued. I still could not do anything myself, which was aggravated by the side effects of the painkillers and nerve tranquilizers. Because of the drugs, I could not think clearly anymore. My weirdest experience was that occasionally my mouth formulated different words than the ones I wanted to say. When trying to read, the letters would jump up and down. I thought to myself, "How can I relate to God when I cannot read His Word?"

In the first year, when the pain got worse instead of better, I wanted to give up. However, I remembered Bible verses about not giving up, having peace of mind, and the promise of healing. Through standing on these promises, I retrieved my peace and started experiencing healing in my body. Step by step my health improved while my faith in God and His Word provided me with the strength to go on. God's promises literally manifested in my life. Diligently studying the Bible and meditating on God's Word generates noticeable results, even in an unexpected future of being incapable to read the Bible.

Being unable to participate actively in my relationship with God, I had no choice than to completely surrender to Him. I comprehended that the relationship is not by my efforts, but by God's. I recognized that I had prided myself in my Bible reading and had believed that my relationship with God depended on me. I became relaxed in my relationship with God, and I learned to accept that God loves me, no matter what, and that He stays with me even if I cannot communicate with Him. And even when I cannot read the Bible, God still relates with me.

Furthermore, I learned to reach out for assistance in everything without feeling ashamed. It is not a sign of weakness when you need help. After all, if I cannot ask for help, then what am I telling God? Am I telling Him that I can do everything by myself and do not need Him? I discovered that asking God and others for help reflects true faith and dependence on God. Through it all, I learned to truly surrender to and trust in God.

After more than two years of pain and incapacitation, I emerged knowing God on a deeper level and depending on Him more than ever before. It is in the worst time of your life that you truly get to know God and His preserving love for you.

Therefore, do not give up when you are in a physically and mentally terrifying situation; just know that it is temporary. Draw your strength from God's Word, which is true and life-giving. Claim God's promises and see the manifestation thereof being realized in your life. Then, focus on your progress, not on your limitations. Rejoice in every step forward. Trust God in everything. He holds you. He will never give up on you. He is with you.

* * *

Christel Owoo passionately believes that you will live a fulfilling life by applying the Word of God to everyday issues. That way, you will reach the full potential God has given you. Her books speak of life-changing encounters and second chances when you follow, obey, and apply God's Word.

45

UNDIAGNOSED

BY JEANETTE GREEN

"No man is an island," I have been told. But for the past seven years, I have been one. And not the idyllic holiday destination kind of island. My life was shipwrecked, and I was washed onto a cannibal-infested island.

These were my "Job" years: three years of torment from mental disease followed by years of suffering from chronic pain. Financial ruin was never far.

These were years of curling up in the dog bed, in the bath, somewhere low, because that was where I belonged. On the floor.

I was discarded human waste.

Blinded by tears, I ran away to nowhere and ended up, for three weeks, in the hospital. The psychiatrist and the psychologist had no name to give my fractured heart. They tried to medicate and talk me out of a haze of oblivion. Instead, they amplified my darkness.

Then followed the pain. The monster devoured my flesh, my life, but was invisible to the best and worst of doctors. They tried naming this pain. Ruptured disc. Chronic gastritis. Fatty liver. Each time there was a name, this monster shook it off, moved elsewhere in my body. A swollen knee. Swollen, sore knuckles. Ribs so tender I could not wear a bra. In my sleep, something happened to me. My tongue slipped under my teeth, and I could not breathe.

I was desperate for a diagnosis, for validation of my pain. It wasn't all in my head! So, I turned to Christian counselors who pointed me to Jesus.

And He began healing me in my dreams.

"Leave your fractured heart with Me," He said. "Repairing it will be a delicate operation. It will take time. First, I must neutralize the poison already in your system. Next, I will remove the thorn, then reconstruct your soul."

He showed me hidden parts of my soul, helped me understand my pain.

A journey of tears, of screaming, of flinging strings of profanity into the air, of singing heart-songs and being held by Jesus, began. Slowly, the light emanating from Him dispelled the darkness within.

At the end of 2020, the years of doctors' visits and hospital stays climaxed in a death sentence being felled over me—one not connected to any of the symptoms I had been experiencing, though. A tiny, flower-shaped blob above my left knee that, they said, would kill me.

Finally, I had a diagnosis. But the doctors' faces were carved with worry. They could do nothing.

Again, Jesus was there. Not in the way I wanted Him to be, not miraculously sweeping away the pain. No. He pulled me into an intimate, slow dance. Called me to walk each day by faith. His grace would carry me, and I would live every day He planned for me, no matter what they said.

It turned out my island was Malta. Storms shipwrecked my life, and snakes tried to latch onto my hand. But I could overcome that. God's promises for my future kept me safe. I would live, do the good works God had prepared for me until I was done. Sometimes, my faith hung by a thread. I failed to shake myself free. That is when I clung to my sword and let my Sword-giver do the slashing. Snakes fled.

God is sovereign, and He is my healer. He could choose to heal through medicine, or He could say one word. That is, if He wanted to heal me, partially, and prolong my life in this world.

Death, I could look forward to. I would return to my homeland where there would be no more tears, no more pain, ever, for me. And I would see God, face to face.

There were others shipwrecked with me. Many suffered from unnamed pain that had doctors scratching their heads. Other sufferers scraped cents together for groceries and could not afford doctors or medicine. If my eyes were on Jesus, I could see in His eyes their pain with my own. I could let His love flow through me to them. My pain became a blessing because before my scars, I had no idea what a life of tears was. And I loved pleasure more than peace.

The same Wind that blew me onto the rocks brought me a new ship. I lost the life I envisaged for myself and instead gained the one God had planned for me.

As I sailed forth, I saw the horizon darken, and soon I was caught up in the mother of all storms—a global one. Still, my ship was not tossed to and fro, and I had light all the way. Those shipwrecked with me I saw sailing alongside me. They had peace, had light, too. Our Creator had prepared our ships.

We would sail safely, carrying His light until He brought us to the heavenly shore.

* * *

Jeanette Green has a heart for Jesus and His heart for her as she writes. In the process, Jesus speaks healing over her. Some of

His words she blogs at www.kardeshae.org. Her novel, *Through Storms with His Words*, is a dream-diary story based on her testimony, which she hopes to publish soon.

46

AFTERMATH OF SHOWING UP

BY JOE S. KIMBROUGH II

*O*n August 29, 2005, I drive south on Interstate 20/59 to Tuscaloosa, Alabama, from my hometown of Leeds. An email from Loyola University New Orleans alerts me to a week's closure of my first undergraduate school. With only a week off, I decide that I can do some service at a refugee center on the University of Alabama's campus. I can, at the very least, show up for bottled-water duty.

Upon my arrival, I park in the only remaining parking spot at the softball compound. The sun bakes the concrete all the way to the recreation center. Then, I nearly smack the welcome table with the front door. After a quick recovery, a fellow undergrad asks, "Hi, are you from New Orleans or here to help?"

The TV across the room grabs my attention. CNN already broadcasts live from the scene of shattered glass and vanished roofs. Without looking at the young man behind the welcome table, I answer, "Both." He stammers over a welcome before offering directions to the student organizations.

I cross the room with a blank nametag and focus still on the TV. One camera travels down St. Charles Avenue in New

Orleans. More damage lines both sides of the road. However, it turns before a shot of Loyola. I reach the table for the Christian organizations without a glimpse of my school or my apartment.

Blessedly, the table puts a wall between the reports and me. I answer the pastor's questions with far more coherence than at the welcome table. The pastor says, "You're exactly what we need. You can share their stories, so do me a favor: Take a thing of water and go to the couches. Pray with anyone in the mood." My eyes blink at the assignment, but I gladly follow my instructions.

Morning fades into afternoon with little more than that. I find a seat near the back and share the moment. Others see their homes or favorite haunts, and I share my experiences in those places. We eat lunch together over tales of work and family. The devastation is always before us, but shared memories create a place of comfort. Still, I see no view of my places.

The flood breaks in the middle of the afternoon. Cameras in helicopters show feet of water from Lake Pontchartrain to the river. Everyone, including the other volunteers, stop with a collective gasp. Silence reigns.

At last, the steeple of Loyola's church peaks above the water. Moments later, two floors of my apartment building poke from the depths. I see three years of work for my scholarship push down the river. Promises of academic conference presentations join the detritus floating to the Gulf of Mexico. The space for my explorations of this world by God's grace disappears beneath the waves.

Amid my contemplations, a young lady taps me on the shoulder. "A local business sent some sandwiches. Would you help pass them out?" she says.

"Yes," I say. "As long as I can go to the gym. I shouldn't watch more of this. Besides, I did show up to help."

A half smile emerges through her pursed lips. She only says, "I understand."

My steps match hers after a brief nod, and I pass out sandwiches with bags of chips for the next hour. In the gym, rows of cots spread across the eight full-sized basketball courts. Each person has a story, and I listen to each one. Most ask for a prayer before taking the food. My last dinner boxes find a middle-aged couple in motorcycle t-shirts and ripped blue jeans.

They use the city as the starting point for visiting all fifty states. I share my dream of doing the same. We talk of prior adventures, and I learn of several common destinations. Before I bless the food as requested, the lady sees one of my rings.

She tells me that she had one very similar to it. The ring is nothing special, but her eyes never leave the ring during my prayer. So, I give her the ring. I say with the first smile all day, "Well, I guess, really, the city has set us upon another great adventure," and I leave. At the end of the row, I look back. They already have maps on their knees, pointing to their next stops.

Throughout that day, God put me where I needed to be. The temptation to despair was great, but His grace was greater. I started the day with a decision to show up. Surely, that became the theme, as others told me what to do. In truth, I suppose that "showing up" is ninety percent of our Christian adventures. What grace from God could we witness if we just show up?

***

Joe S. Kimbrough II writes mostly Christian fiction from his home north of Birmingham, Alabama. Stories make the space for unfettered time in God's presence, creating an openness to His call for our lives. Go to jskimbroughii.com for more stories and reflections.

47

OFFERING HOPE TO PEOPLE WHO NEED GOD

BY JIM JONES WITH RICHARD GREENE, 2ND PLACE WINNER

*J*ust as Linda and I had enjoyed so many previous fun-filled family vacations to Disney World, we anticipated that our umpteenth visit would be another wild adventure.

Whoa, were we caught off guard!

And our world would be rocked once again six months later. And yet, God was creating in that stretch in 2008 a tapestry that we could never have envisioned or orchestrated on our own. He turned our trials into triumphs—with a unique twist. The Lord was not only working in our hearts and transforming us more into His likeness, but He was also revealing His master plan to redirect our golden years to invest them to feed hungry children and families in Central Alabama.

Those were not easy days. But with God, all things are possible.

Our opening day at Disney went off without a hitch. Before the crack of dawn, though, day two would begin with a horrific headache and severe gastric symptoms. I couldn't focus or think straight.

Poking Linda with my elbow, I said, "I've got a problem. Something's terribly wrong. I need help."

Linda, a veteran hospital-floor and surgical nurse, jumped into action. She called a taxi to get us to a nearby emergency clinic. Assessing that my blood pressure was abnormally high, the doctor on duty called for an ambulance to rush me to a stroke/cardiac center next to Epcot at Disney.

I was suffering a TIA, a minor stroke. The staff provided world-class care to me and to Linda as well.

Two days there were followed by additional care at the University Medical Center in Birmingham, Alabama, just one hour from our home in Sylacauga.

When I finally got home forty-eight hours later, I faced tough choices. I fully recovered with one huge exception, and I mean huge: I couldn't remember everything about being a nurse anesthetist. That wouldn't work! I had envisioned working another two to five years, but instead, I had to hang up my scrubs after a wonderful career I had reveled in ever since my Vietnam War days.

Wow, Linda and I could now visit our family and keep going on mission trips that we had done for years to Africa and Central America. And spend lots of time fishing on our new eighteen-foot bass boat!

Later that year, we had to hurry to Cincinnati, Ohio, with one of our sons and daughter-in-law, who were seeking medical help to treat a troubled pregnancy. While there, Linda and I attended a church service we had picked out randomly from the phone book. Tony Fairhead, the guest speaker, shared about his local food ministry.

"There's somebody here who needs to be doing something about feeding hungry children where they live," he said toward the end of his message. "And that person is you!"

We gulped. Tony's finger was pointing directly at us. I slunk down into my pew.

Linda and I had seen hunger in Kenya, Dominican Republic, Honduras, and elsewhere. But we had no idea what to do about it in Central Alabama. We didn't have the knowledge. We certainly didn't have the money.

So, to be honest, we ran from God! We resisted for about two years. But He wouldn't leave us alone. I can't recall how many sleepless nights I experienced, wrestling with this decision, crying out to God for answers.

We prayed. We scoured the Scriptures. We sought out counsel, including from Tony Fairhead, whose finger touched off this search. He gave us solid suggestions about how to launch out.

Finally, Linda and I believed God was leading us to dive into the deep end, trusting Him. We started small, passing out forty bags, filled with food we had purchased, to people living in a local housing complex. We then heard about teachers who were using their own resources to feed hungry students at their schools. Our hearts broke. Linda and I took them on. Eventually, we expanded our outreach to include families.

Today, by God's grace, we stand in awe of how God has consistently answered our prayers to provide the funds and the volunteers to help feed more than 2,200 children every weekend and nearly 900 families each month. But not just to feed them physically. We also insert a Life Event Card in each bag. These include a Bible verse and a few sentences that encourage people and point them to Jesus.

Linda and I are not superheroes. We're just ordinary Christians who follow an extraordinary God. We're grateful that He brought trials into our lives and gave us the grace to triumph to serve Him with joy and offer His hope to people who need Him!

***

Jim Jones served forty-six years as a nurse anesthetist in Sylacauga, Alabama, retiring in 2008. God then led him and his wife, Linda, into a feeding ministry two years later. The couple founded Alabama Childhood Food Solutions and they together —along with 500 volunteers—serve hungry children and families in Central Alabama. Jim and Linda are members of Double Oak Community Church in Mount Laurel, Alabama, and they have six adult children, seventeen grandchildren and four great-grandchildren.

Richard Greene retired in 2018 following a forty-two-year journalistic career. He had the joy of traveling to more than sixty countries, reporting on what God was doing through The Navigators, Trans World Radio, the Billy Graham Evangelistic Association, and Samaritan's Purse. He's now blogging and editorially volunteering with several Christian ministries. He and his wife, Lynda, are active members of Alliance Bible Fellowship in Boone, North Carolina. They have two adult daughters and three granddaughters.

48

I WAS BLIND BUT NOW I SEE

BY REBECCA S. CARLISLE

My y life was beautiful as I anticipated my upcoming trip to Sweden, Norway, and Thailand with Shea, my daughter. It was a dream trip for me and a working trip for her. She was a senior flight attendant for a major airline, and she often invited me to travel with her. On January 6, 2020, we left from Fort Lauderdale, flying to Sweden on the Dreamliner 787 airplane. All was right with the world.

In Sweden, we visited a working castle. The guide showed us a picture of the king who was known to walk through the castle on a regular basis. He lived in a castle outside the city, and this castle served as his office. I watched, hoping to catch a glimpse of the king.

Norway, with enchanting scenery and the sapphire-colored skies, was magical. I walked on the beautiful beaches of Thailand and shopped in the local marketplace, enjoying the friendly, gentle people. I marveled how much we were alike, yet from very different backgrounds and countries.

As I was busy planning my next trip, I was completely unaware of what was festering in other parts of the world. I did not realize something could disrupt and destroy every part of our existence. This would be the last time I would travel out of the country. The airline would eventually go bankrupt, and their planes would be grounded.

In fewer than two months, people all over the world would be dying at an alarming rate with hospitals filled to capacity. Refrigerated trucks outside hospitals would be used to store the deceased, our loved ones, in body bags. People would be left to die without family members to console them. Schools, churches, and universities would close their doors to stop the spread of the virus, or at least to slow it down. Nursing homes would be closed to visitors for fear it would infect the residents and kill them. Family's livelihoods would end as businesses closed. People would be desperate to find food to feed their families.

Churches would soon open with safeguards in place. The first Sunday, I ventured out wearing my mask and practicing social distancing. It felt good to be back in a church building. Afterwards, I stayed for Sunday school. It was during Sunday school I had a revelation and discovered my greatest tragedy.

My teacher, Jerry Prince, asked, "What is the greatest tragedy in the world today?" I immediately knew it was the pandemic. COVID-19 was the worst thing, and I could not imagine anything worse. But I was wrong.

Jerry described the greatest tragedy in the world was the mistreatment of God's Word by Christians and sinners. Jerry was referring to the sermon notes of his great uncle, Reverend Pat Johnson, who served as pastor of Roopville Baptist in the 1950s. The sermon was over seventy years old but still relevant today.

There are three major ways Christians mistreat God's Word, the Bible:

- We neglect God's Word by not reading and studying it.
- We reject God's Word and do not believe it to be the Word of God.
- We correct God's Word and change it to fit our situation.

Pandemics, plagues, and disasters have been around since the beginning of time. The Bible is a blueprint to live by and follow.

By reading and studying the Bible, I am happier and at peace with what God has planned for me. The pandemic is a tragic event, but, as a Christian, it is reassuring and comforting to know God is in control and in charge. I meditate on Scriptures, and they give me hope. Non-Christians look to Christians for answers in dealing with tragedies. As a Christian, let's show the world how to find peace by using the Bible, God's Word, as a guide.

My worst tragedy was not what I had thought. Once I discovered the real problem, I could then face the pandemic and anything else life might throw my way. As a Christian, I live by the following:

- God loves me and sent His Son to die so I could have eternal life.
- Nothing is impossible for God, He can do all things, and He is the Creator of the universe.
- God is in control, and nothing is a surprise to Him.
- I trust and love God with all my heart and soul.
- I can do all things through God who gives me strength.
- I believe the Bible to be the Word of God.

Knowing God, and knowing Jesus as my Savior, is the answer to every tragedy. Knowing God as my Savior is knowing the greatest joy, peace, and contentment in my life. The Bible is the Word of God. Tell the world how they can have the same peace, joy, and contentment because Jesus loves them and died for them.

* * *

Rebecca S. Carlisle lives in Roopville, Georgia. She was an educator/administrator for forty-one years, serving as principal of Ephesus Elementary before retiring. She has two grown daughters, Samantha and Paige ("Shea"). Since retiring, she has written articles for *Lifetouch* and Christian Focus Publishers. Rebecca's published books include *52 Hats, A Memoir; A Legend in His Time: John W. Cox; Sharing Lives: A Tale of Two Kidneys;* and *The Divine Touch: Thirteen Spectacular Accounts of Supernatural Healing.*

49

THE SWORD

BY LARRY MANCE

The happenings in Alex's life had troubled him for quite some time, but now he faced a genuine crisis. He wondered if he was cursed, having been plagued by circumstances that defied explanation. He had come to the end of his rope. "Something had to give."

Running away, quitting, and taking his life seemed to be viable choices. Suicide is high on the list of Christian taboos, "but what the heck?" God wasn't listening to his prayers anyway. A baptized believer, the core of his beliefs shook, causing him to question God's reality.

He decided to visit his friend Charles Smith, a retired pharmacist in Toccoa, Georgia. Charles's insight had helped him in the past—non-judgmental insight and elderly wisdom had saved him, preventing him from making costly, youthful mistakes.

He traveled to the Northeast Georgia mountains through Currahee Mountain. As a teenager, he often went mountaintop to pray and seek God's face. He was long overdue for a visit with God.

"Lord," he prayed, "my soul is weary. I need a divine intervention to keep from giving up." He went into the sleepy town to find his Caucasian friend, thirty years older than he.

He shared his emotions and pain with Charles. Then Charles told him the story of a young man who had had a similar experience.

"To say that Itsume was born under a bad sign would be somewhat sacrilegious," Charles said, "and an understatement." Nothing came easy, and he was always warring to complete simple tasks. He became a soldier in Vietnam, a war he did not approve of, but he believed sacrificing himself for his family amounted to the greater good, therefore making it justifiable. He married in college then a year later, he enlisted in the Air Force.

In a small third world village outside Manila, frying in the morning heat, tears raining down his cheeks, he sat in the marketplace beside an old Filipino man. Unable to bear his unquenchable pain, he cried out until pain robbed his vocal cords of sound. Weeping and death had taken a hiatus. He felt compelled to share his feelings with the old man and began talking about emotional pain endured as a child by a father who punished him severely. He started to work at seven because his dad wouldn't buy his toys, school clothes, or insurance. He attempted suicide at age nine, trying to down himself in the neighborhood swimming pool.

He recalled integrating the public school in 1965, at the age of fourteen, and feeling like a leper. No one would talk to him, and his teachers ignored him. At age sixteen, his cousin stabbed him with a butcher knife in the throat, almost severing his windpipe.

The old man turned to him, speaking in English. "So it is in the life of a man whom God chooses to use," he said. "The Blacksmith of the Universe will place you on the Anvil of Life and take the Hammer of Circumstance, beating and knocking you into shape. He then takes you off the anvil and plunges you into the burning hot coals of trials and disappointments. He places you back on the anvil, hammering, knocking, and beating you until He determines you've learned what He's trying to teach you, until your response is consistent with His Word and Christ's teachings. After being tried by fire, He dips you into cold water to forge you with relief. He brings you out of the water, and you have become a well-forged polished sword, unbreakable, ready to engage the enemy in battle.

Itsume's eyes opened. He understood. "To him that much is given much is required." "All things work together for good for them that Love the Lord and are called according to His purpose." "Though He may slay me yet will I trust Him." It all made sense—what God had been up to. Itsume's sadness changed to joy. God had chosen him. God had been there for him the whole time.

Scripture became clear to him. He might not see or understand it, but God is present, forever doing exceedingly abundantly above all we might ask or think. At last, every pain had meaning. He found comfort knowing God had orchestrated the events of his life for a greater good. He would trust and wait on Him. He would buckle his "seatbelt of trust" and hang on for the ride.

So, go forth grasshopper. Be the sword God created you to be. His eye is on the sparrow and on you, too. Alex never questioned God again. He simply "buckled his seatbelt" and, with determination and excitement, served and followed Him, eager to be transformed into Christ's image.

* * *

Larry Mance is the author of *Teachable Moments* and *Bedtime Stories for Grown-Ups*, two collections of Christian short stories.

He earned his degree from the Georgia Institute of Technology, having enrolled as one of only sixty-five Black students. Mance is an Air Force veteran and is currently completing his autobiography.

QUESTIONS FOR PERSONAL REFLECTION/GROUP STUDY

Dear reader:

In this section, we invite you to participate with us by telling your own story of tragedy and healing. The questions are meant to help you think, ponder, and reflect upon life, faith, and hope.

You may use these questions, thoughts, and Scriptures in a personal way, alone in your study, or you may invite a group of believers to join you in this study. The questions are designed to allow you to share your own story with others if you wish to, seeking help and hope through the fellowship of other believers. You may wish to begin a time of Bible Study using these questions and thoughts as a springboard to opening up conversation, sharing stories, helping in your own or another's healing.

We suggest you record your reflections within the space reserved for you in these pages, and, if more space is needed, to write your thoughts on additional paper.

Feel free to refrain from voicing your opinion if you study within a group. Some of the questions are intimate and personal, and you may not feel comfortable sharing this deeply.

QUESTIONS FOR PERSONAL REFLECTION/GROUP STUDY

May God richly bless you as you continue in this special Bible Study.

Tragedies in Your Own Life

In your own life, what tragedies have you experienced that threatened to overwhelm you?

_____
_____
_____
_____

How have these tragedies affected you and changed your life?

_____
_____
_____
_____

How did your faith in God through Jesus Christ help you to cope, conquer, and overcome your tragedy, turning it into a triumph?

_____
_____
_____
_____

What painful experiences are you now suffering?

_____
_____
_____
_____

QUESTIONS FOR PERSONAL REFLECTION/GROUP STUDY

How are these experiences changing your life?

_____
_____
_____
_____

What are your most urgent needs right now, and how can a fellow believer pray for you?

_____
_____
_____
_____

Have you sensed and felt God's presence as you've suffered through a tragedy? In what ways?

_____
_____
_____
_____

Did you experience a time in your suffering when you felt God was distant or absent? If so, would you please explain?

_____
_____
_____
_____

Have you been able to use past tragedies and triumphs to help others who are suffering the same types of experiences? If so, in what ways?

_____
_____
_____
_____

QUESTIONS FOR PERSONAL REFLECTION/GROUP STUDY

What is your definition of a "wounded healer"?

_____
_____
_____
_____

Does your own healing and triumph enable you to become a "wounded healer" to another person? If so, how?

_____
_____
_____
_____

What valuable lessons did you learn as you journeyed through your tragedy?

_____
_____
_____
_____

Tragedies in Your Family's Lives

What tragedies have occurred (or are occurring) in the life of your family?

_____
_____
_____
_____

QUESTIONS FOR PERSONAL REFLECTION/GROUP STUDY

What effect has this tragedy had on you personally? On your family members?
_____
_____
_____
_____

How has this tragedy affected your family's day to day life and future?
_____
_____
_____
_____

Is the tragedy pulling your family apart or strengthening the family unit? Why? How?
_____
_____
_____
_____

Are your family members depending on God to help them through the tragedy? If so, how and in what ways?
_____
_____
_____
_____

QUESTIONS FOR PERSONAL REFLECTION/GROUP STUDY

Do you have a concern for a family member who is suffering and might not know the salvation of Jesus Christ? Would you please describe your concerns?

_____
_____
_____
_____

How have past specific tragedies in your family's lives affected your family? Would you please describe?

_____
_____
_____
_____

Would you please describe your family's journey to wholeness and healing?

_____
_____
_____
_____

The Tragedies and Triumphs of Others

These questions are taken specifically from some of the stories written in the book. You might wish to choose to reflect on the stories you can most identify with.

A Newborn's Disease and Death

Please read Hayden Walker's story, "Zoe Karis." Hayden describes experiencing "moments of utter brokenness" as she awaits her dying unborn daughter's delivery.

QUESTIONS FOR PERSONAL REFLECTION/GROUP STUDY

In what ways can you identify with this young mother? Have you experienced a similar loss?

How did Hayden find strength in the midst of such sorrow?

Why did Hayden name her baby girl *Zoe*?

When you read Hayden's story, how did it affect you emotionally and spiritually?

If you could speak personally with Hayden, what would you say to her, what questions might you ask her?

QUESTIONS FOR PERSONAL REFLECTION/GROUP STUDY

A Life-Changing Stroke

Please read Jim Jones's story, "Offering Hope to People Who Need God." Jim describes his pain, stroke, and loss of a lifetime career he loved.

Have you or a family member faced a similar loss? Would you please describe it?

_____
_____
_____
_____

How did you cope during the tragedy, and how did it change your life and your family's lives?

_____
_____
_____
_____

How did you triumph over your loss?

_____
_____
_____
_____

Did your faith in Christ point you toward healing? Would you please explain how?

_____
_____
_____
_____

QUESTIONS FOR PERSONAL REFLECTION/GROUP STUDY

How did God step into Jim and Linda's lives and use their tragedy for good? In what ways did their lives become incredibly useful to God for feeding Alabama's hungry children?

_____
_____
_____
_____

If you could speak personally with Jim, what would you say to him, what questions might you ask him?

_____
_____
_____
_____

A Husband's Workplace Injury

Please read Terrie Todd's story, "Living with a One-Armed Man." She describes her husband's workplace injury and how it forever changed their lives.

Have you or a family member experienced this type of loss from an accident? If so, would you please describe it?

_____
_____
_____
_____

How did the disability change your day-to-day life, your family's lives?

_____
_____
_____
_____

QUESTIONS FOR PERSONAL REFLECTION/GROUP STUDY

How did you come to a state of acceptance, cope with the trauma, and find emotional and physical healing?

_____
_____
_____
_____

Did the experience strengthen your relationship with God? Would you please explain how and why?

_____
_____
_____
_____

Have you adjusted to the painful tragedy? In what ways have you found healing and triumph?

_____
_____
_____
_____

If you could speak personally with Terrie, what would you say to her, what questions might you ask her?

_____
_____
_____
_____

A Father's Illness and Death

Please read Alberta Sequeira's story, "Time Waits for No One." Alberta describes how her father's cancer devastated his life, as well as her own. She, her mother, and her family watched him

QUESTIONS FOR PERSONAL REFLECTION/GROUP STUDY

suffer extreme pain, live sedated with morphine, and go in and out of consciousness.

Have you ever lost a parent to cancer? If so, please explain. How did you cope as you watched your loved one suffer and die? Did the experience strengthen your faith in God or distance you from Him? What has happened to you, your family, and your faith since the trauma?

_____
_____
_____
_____
_____
_____
_____

What other tragedies did Alberta experience in her life?

_____
_____
_____
_____

How did the sickness and death of Alberta's father—as well as her other tragedies—change her faith and bring her back to God?

_____
_____
_____
_____

QUESTIONS FOR PERSONAL REFLECTION/GROUP STUDY

Do you agree with Alberta when she writes, "Miracles do happen. God never closes the door on us. We are the ones who have to open our hearts to let Him into our soul"? Why or why not?

_____
_____
_____
_____

If you could speak personally with Alberta, what would you say to her, what questions might you ask her?

_____
_____
_____
_____

An Abusive Childhood

Please read Chizobah Mary Alintah's story, "My Resentment Disappeared." Chizobah grew up with a father she describes as "my destroyer," a man who "stripped me of my childhood." Chizobah became a "wanderer" whom men found easy to abuse. After many horrific experiences, feeling "depressed and dejected," she vowed never to trust men again.

Did you suffer an abusive childhood, hurt by the ones who are supposed to love and protect you? If so, would you like to describe it? How did their abuse affect you? How did you find healing? What happened to your faith during the pain and after the healing?

_____
_____
_____
_____

QUESTIONS FOR PERSONAL REFLECTION/GROUP STUDY

_____
_____
_____
_____

How did Chizobah find healing from a lifetime of continued trauma?

_____
_____
_____
_____

What did Chizobah learn about Jesus her "Savior"?

_____
_____
_____
_____

What life-changing decision did Chizobah make in order to find the healing she needed?

_____
_____
_____
_____

If you could speak personally with Chizobah, what would you say to her, what questions might you ask her?

_____
_____
_____
_____

QUESTIONS FOR PERSONAL REFLECTION/GROUP STUDY

A Spouse's Mental Illness

Please read Richelle Hatton's story, "The River of Life." Richelle married a man who had deep mental illness issues and spent time in a hospital psychiatric ward. She writes, "I felt lost. I had no road map for dealing with mental illness and recovery." Together, Richelle and her husband, Stephen, battled his mental illness.

Have you ever battled a spouse's mental illness? If so, would you like to explain?

_____
_____
_____
_____

How did your spouse's mental illness affect you, your marriage, and your family?

_____
_____
_____
_____

How did you, your spouse, your family, and your marriage find healing?

_____
_____
_____
_____

QUESTIONS FOR PERSONAL REFLECTION/GROUP STUDY

What did Richelle learn about God as she and her husband journeyed through the trauma of mental issues and psychiatric wards?

_____
_____
_____
_____

How did they find healing?

_____
_____
_____
_____

If you could speak personally with Richelle, what would you say to her, what questions might you ask her?

_____
_____
_____
_____

Personal Undiagnosed Pain

Please read Esther M. Bandy's story, "Don't Ask *Why*, Ask *What*." Esther suffered extreme personal physical pain from an unknown illness, one that interfered with her and her husband's missionary work in Mexico. She writes, "I often had headaches and abdominal pain, and sometimes vomiting and weakness. At times, I was too weak to get out of bed or move my body." Doctors could offer Esther no diagnosis. Esther often asked "Why, Lord? What's wrong with me?" and begged God to heal her. For years, disabled and homebound, Esther prayed for relief.

QUESTIONS FOR PERSONAL REFLECTION/GROUP STUDY

Are you currently suffering personal affliction from an undiagnosed physical disease or condition? If so, would you please explain.

_____
_____
_____
_____

How are you coping with physical pain?

_____
_____
_____
_____

How are you experiencing God's presence in the midst of personal pain?

_____
_____
_____
_____

In what ways did personal physical pain change Esther's life and work?

_____
_____
_____
_____

What did Esther discover about God's presence in her suffering, and how did she find triumph through accepting her pain in the light of God's perfect plan?

_____
_____
_____

QUESTIONS FOR PERSONAL REFLECTION/GROUP STUDY

Esther felt blessed and strengthened by the Scripture found in Psalm 119:71: "It is good for me that I have been afflicted; that I might learn thy statutes." Has Scripture been a source of strength to you in your illness, and if so, what verses have most helped you?

_____
_____
_____
_____

If you could speak personally with Esther, what would you say to her, what questions might you ask her?

_____
_____
_____
_____

Personal Molestation

Please read Emma Bloor's story, "Frost in My Soul." As a child, Emma endured a traumatic incident of abuse and personal molestation. For years, she suffered, keeping the tragedy a painful secret. "For years," she writes, "I denied [that my abuser's horrific act] affected my relationships, my trust, and my ability to be intimate with anyone. Even God." Emma finally found healing from her trauma, and with God's help, she forgave her rapist.

Have you ever experienced a trauma like Emma suffered? If so, how did it affect and change you?

_____
_____
_____
_____

QUESTIONS FOR PERSONAL REFLECTION/GROUP STUDY

Have you been able to heal, find relief from your pain, and forgive the abuser? If so, would you like to describe your healing?

_____
_____
_____
_____

What did this type of trauma—the pain of another's abuse—have on your relationship with other people? With your spouse? With God?

_____
_____
_____
_____

Would you please describe your life now, after finding God's healing and help?

_____
_____
_____
_____

If you could speak personally with Emma, what would you say to her, what questions might you ask her?

_____
_____
_____
_____

A Caregiver's Battle with Her Mother's Alzheimer's Disease

Please read Cheryl Schuermann's story, "I Hear Him." Cheryl became the primary caregiver for her mother who suffered from the last stages of Alzheimer's disease. She writes, "My heart broke for her [her mother] so many times, I wondered if it would recover." While managing her mother's fragile, declining health, Cheryl experienced her own autoimmune challenges. "The responsibility of making every detailed decision for another adult's life took its toll both emotionally and physically," Cheryl writes. "I often felt helpless, hopeless, and angry at the ugliness of the disease." Cheryl found emotional, heart-healing through God's Word and promises.

Have you ever served as a caregiver for someone you loved, for someone suffering the devastation of debilitating brain disease and dementia caused by Alzheimer's disease? If so, would you please describe?

_____
_____
_____
_____

What heartaches, like Cheryl, did you experience as you cared for your loved one?

_____
_____
_____
_____

Did you sense God's presence during these tragic times? Please explain.

_____
_____
_____
_____

QUESTIONS FOR PERSONAL REFLECTION/GROUP STUDY

How did you find healing? If you are in the midst of the trauma, how are you journeying toward healing?

_____
_____
_____
_____

What practical advice would you give another person caring for a loved one with Alzheimer's disease?

_____
_____
_____
_____

Cheryl found healing, and was greatly helped by Scripture, especially Psalm 46:10: "Be still, and know that I am God." She writes, "He [God] will win the battle, even in the midst of pain and suffering and heartbreak."

In what ways, in the midst of your own painful experience, can you identify with Cheryl and her caregiving pain and her healing?

_____
_____
_____
_____

If you could speak personally with Cheryl, what would you say to her, what questions might you ask her?

_____
_____
_____
_____

QUESTIONS FOR PERSONAL REFLECTION/GROUP STUDY

Sudden Physical Disability

Please read Christel Owoo's story, "Surrender." Christel, a hardworking and independent woman, leaned forward causing an excruciating pain in her lower back. "I screamed and tried to move," she writes, "but ... my back was 'locked-up.'" Physically disabled and suffering intense pain, Christel imagined herself "paralyzed for the rest of my life." The spine injury left her unable to work in her church and her job. She could no longer perform simple household chores nor lift/carry her toddler son. "A journey of extreme pain, physical disability, and sedating medication ensued," she writes. Christel suffered disability and pain for years, but throughout her trauma, she discovered God's deep love and healing.

Do you now, or have you ever, suffered a physically disability that interfered with your day-to-day life and future? If so, would you please explain?

Did you sense and depend upon God's presence in your pain? If so, in what ways?

QUESTIONS FOR PERSONAL REFLECTION/GROUP STUDY

If you found relief and healing, please describe how you found it. If not, please describe how you accepted and learned to live with your disability?

_____
_____
_____
_____

Would you please describe how the painful disability changed your relationship with God?

_____
_____
_____
_____

After more than two years of physical pain, incapacitation, and terror, Christel "emerged knowing God on a deeper level and depending on Him more than ever before." In your opinion, what can we, as Christians, learn from Christel Owoo's story?

_____
_____
_____
_____

If you could speak personally with Christel, what would you say to her, what questions might you ask her?

_____
_____
_____
_____

QUESTIONS FOR PERSONAL REFLECTION/GROUP STUDY

A Father's Suicide

Please read Linda Marie's story, "To Err Is Human." After Linda's eighteenth birthday, her severely depressed father, a Navy pilot, killed himself. "At the time of my dad's death," Linda writes, "I was devastated and felt abandoned by both my earthly and heavenly Father." The suicide left her mother wrestling with extreme anger, and she threw Linda out of her house. Linda was forced to drop out of college and live with a neighbor. She later built a business and married, but she discovered that her husband had a drug problem and cheated on her with other women. Linda experienced a remarkable recovery from her life's tragedies as she pulled close to God and allowed Him to love and teach her.

A parent's suicide can cripple a son or daughter. Have you ever endured such a tragedy in your own life? If so, would you explain what happened and how you coped with the loss and aftermath?

_____
_____
_____
_____

Do you know of someone close to you who might be depressed and discouraged, and who is possibly contemplating suicide? If so, have you been able to speak with and help the person? In what ways?

_____
_____
_____
_____

QUESTIONS FOR PERSONAL REFLECTION/GROUP STUDY

In your opinion, why did Linda's tragedy make her feel abandoned by both her father and her heavenly Father?
_____
_____
_____
_____

What brought about Linda's healing, not only her father's tragic suicide, but the other tragedies she suffered in her young life?
_____
_____
_____
_____

How did God love and protect Linda, and what was her response to Him?
_____
_____
_____
_____

If you could speak personally with Linda, what would you say to her, what questions might you ask her?
_____
_____
_____
_____

Divorce

Please read Cheryl Gore Pollard's story, "Despair to Repair." Divorce is the end of a marriage, a union. Divorce in this country happens to about fifty percent of first marriages, and to more than seventy-five percent of second and third marriages.

QUESTIONS FOR PERSONAL REFLECTION/GROUP STUDY

After a long, struggling marriage, Cheryl chose to divorce her husband and begin a new life. She writes, "The process of divorce was long and devastating, even with God's guidance. Accusations, threats, disappointment."

Have you suffered the trauma of a struggling marriage and a devastating divorce? If so, what did you learn throughout the process?

_____
_____
_____
_____

Did you sense God's help and presence during the ordeal? If so, in what ways? Did you become closer to Him or did the divorce distance you in your relationship to God? Would you like to explain your situation and the effect it had on your faith?

_____
_____
_____
_____
_____
_____
_____
_____

What is your opinion of Cheryl's decision to divorce her husband?

_____
_____
_____
_____

QUESTIONS FOR PERSONAL REFLECTION/GROUP STUDY

What lessons did Cheryl learn as she went through the "devastating" process of divorce?

_____
_____
_____
_____

What internal struggles did Cheryl endure throughout the divorce?

_____
_____
_____
_____

If you could speak personally with Cheryl, what would you say to her, what questions might you ask her?

_____
_____
_____
_____

Terrifying Personal Experiences

Please read Donna Kay's story, "The Shore." Donna lived through a terrifying experience when she and two college friends drifted far out to sea on lightweight rafts while on vacation at the beach. "Fear filled my heart as I gazed at what looked like hundreds of jellyfish below us … it was horrifying!" she writes. Paddling frantically toward shore while enduring painful stings, Donna tried to remain calm. When she watched a shark pass beneath her, her heart sank. She writes, "We are going to die out here." She survived the near-death experience, and her faith in God became stronger.

QUESTIONS FOR PERSONAL REFLECTION/GROUP STUDY

Have you ever experienced a terrifying incident in which you faced the event of your own death? If so, would you please describe?

_____
_____
_____
_____

In the middle of the danger, what thoughts came into your mind?

_____
_____
_____
_____

Did you feel and trust God's presence during the crisis? In what ways did God comfort you?

_____
_____
_____
_____

Did the experience strengthen your faith, and, if so, in what ways?

_____
_____
_____
_____

QUESTIONS FOR PERSONAL REFLECTION/GROUP STUDY

If you could speak personally with Donna, what would you say to her, what questions might you ask her?

_____
_____
_____
_____

A Sick Child and Grandchild

Please read Gayle Childress Greene's story, "Not. That. Story." Gayle's twenty-six-year-old daughter was diagnosed with multiple sclerosis. She feared for her daughter's future. Gayle's first grandchild was born with a rare condition called arthrogryposis multiplex congenita, a disease affecting his arms. She writes, "I tried to have faith, to believe in God's goodness, but I was overwhelmed by fear. I was a mother. I was a fixer. But I couldn't fix this."

Have you ever personally faced a child's tragic diagnosis and illness? If so, how did you respond to the news?

_____
_____
_____
_____

Did you realize God's comfort throughout the experience, and if so, in what ways?

_____
_____
_____
_____

QUESTIONS FOR PERSONAL REFLECTION/GROUP STUDY

How did Gayle depend on God's Word to guide her through her tragedies?

_____
_____
_____
_____

When Gayle read Isaiah 43:2, "When you pass through the waters, I will be with you," how did she receive God's comfort?

_____
_____
_____
_____

Describe the "ray of hope" that warmed Gayle's heart and taught her difficult lessons in her healing.

_____
_____
_____
_____

What did the painful experiences teach Gayle about God, hope, and trust?

_____
_____
_____
_____

If you could speak personally with Gayle, what would you say to her, what questions might you ask her?

_____
_____
_____
_____

QUESTIONS FOR PERSONAL REFLECTION/GROUP STUDY

A Premature Birth, a Tragic Death, and a Father's Faith

Please read Howard Abrams's story, "Jonathan David." When Howard's pregnant wife, Becky, went into unexpected early labor, she delivered a tiny one pound, three-ounce baby boy. Howard writes that doctors told them that "very few infants born at twenty-four weeks survived, and he encouraged us to make funeral plans." Howard describes the emotional roller coaster that took place for the next few months. Their son, Jonathan, died at the hospital when a piece of equipment failed. Later, God blessed the couple with a healthy baby girl.

Have you ever experienced a son or daughter's premature birth and anticipated their upcoming death? If so, would you please explain the experience?

_____
_____
_____
_____

In what ways did you depend on God's help and comfort during that tragedy?

_____
_____
_____
_____

Howard writes that Psalm 121 brought him great comfort when he struggled and felt discouraged. What Scriptures did you cling to in the midst of devastation? How did they help you?

_____
_____
_____
_____

QUESTIONS FOR PERSONAL REFLECTION/GROUP STUDY

How did God guide the healing process for Howard and Becky, and what did they learn from Jonathan in his brief life?

_____
_____
_____
_____

If you could speak personally with Howard, what would you say to him, what questions might you ask him?

_____
_____
_____
_____

Bad Decisions and Forced Abortions

Please read Cecilia James's story, "Rescued by an Angel." Cecilia's childhood was marred by domestic violence. Impoverished, she became involved with a distrustful man who promised to marry her. She became pregnant. She writes, "I was shattered. Never in my life did I experience such conflicting emotions." With her partner's support, she terminated the pregnancy. She became pregnant a second time, and again terminated the pregnancy. When she became pregnant a third time, her partner ordered her to abort the baby. She writes, "For the first time in my life, my naïve eyes opened. I realized that he never had any intention of marrying me ... he had no conscience at all." Cecilia's life turned upside down, and she experienced trauma after painful trauma. She finally reached "rock bottom." She writes, "The good thing about reaching rock bottom is that you realize that the only way out is looking up to God." Out of Cecilia's incredible healing came her remarkable life's ministry.

QUESTIONS FOR PERSONAL REFLECTION/GROUP STUDY

Can you identify with any of the painful experiences Cecilia mentions in her story? If so, which ones? Would you like to share your own story of tragedy?

_____
_____
_____
_____

How did you find healing? Perhaps you are still in your journey toward healing. If so, what part is your faith in God playing to help you heal?

_____
_____
_____
_____

When Cecilia looks back on her tragic life, what is her response to the suffering she endured?

_____
_____
_____
_____

If you could speak personally with Cecilia, what would you say to her, what questions might you ask her?

_____
_____
_____
_____

Infertility

Please read Stephanie Rodda's story, "A Woman Forsaken." Stephanie writes about her longing for a child, suffering two

QUESTIONS FOR PERSONAL REFLECTION/GROUP STUDY

miscarriages, and after ten years of marriage, remaining childless. Stephanie writes, "I felt betrayed by my own body, misunderstood by the people I loved the most, and abandoned by God." God answered Stephanie's prayers not through a pregnancy, but through foster care.

Are you currently experiencing infertility, and if so, what are your thoughts and feelings about the inability to become pregnant?

_____
_____
_____
_____

How did Stephanie's healing happen, and how was that healing orchestrated by God?

_____
_____
_____
_____

How has Stephanie's healing been a source of love, comfort, and protection for dozens of children God has sent into her home and care?

_____
_____
_____
_____

If you could speak personally with Stephanie, what would you say to her, what questions might you ask her?

_____
_____
_____

QUESTIONS FOR PERSONAL REFLECTION/GROUP STUDY

Becoming God's Heart and God's Hands to Hurting Others

We, as Christians, become God's heart and God's hands when we reach out in love and compassion to others who have been wounded by life. By sharing their experiences, these remarkable people have told their intimate stories in book form, hoping to become "wounded healers" to you, and to all those who face their own tragedies and yearn for healing.

In this section, we hope to share some ways that you can reach out, share God's extraordinary love, and help bring healing into the life of another person.

Here are some practical suggestions:

Be present. If possible, spend time with the hurting person, listening, loving, and encouraging her in her faith and life.

Pray for and with the person enduring trauma. The purpose of intercessory prayer is to help friends, family members, and others through difficult times. When you bring a person before God in prayer, be sure to tell the person you are praying for them. Read and study the intercessory prayer in John 17 that Jesus, Himself, prayed for His disciples and for all believers.

Ask others to pray for the hurting person. If situations are told to you in confidence, please do not break that confidence. Request prayer for "unspoken needs," and enlist others to join in prayer for healing.

If possible, **attend to the person's physical needs**. Not everyone can stop their work to become a full-time caregiver, but every little effort you can contribute will help a person undergoing trauma. For instance:

QUESTIONS FOR PERSONAL REFLECTION/GROUP STUDY

- Take prepared food to the person, encouraging them to eat healthy meals. Either cook it yourself or pick it up from a nearby restaurant. Employ restaurants that deliver food.
- Offer to drive the needy person to doctors' appointments, therapy sessions, church services, etc. Enlist others to offer their help in transporting the person to various functions and appointments.
- Send cards and notes regularly to the person, reminding him that he is in your thoughts and prayers, and asking how you might help him.
- Ask your church to help the person financially if lack of money has become a problem. Help pay the person's rent, insurance, medical bills, groceries, medicines, etc.
- Help clean the person's house, especially if they have regular visitors and feel embarrassed over a cluttered, unkept home.
- Run errands. Takes clothes to the cleaners, help transport their children to and from school and afterschool activities, pick up prescriptions and groceries, and do other errands they might not be able to accomplish themselves.
- Babysit small children, especially if a young mother is unable to care for them.
- Help with the person's laundry, washing, drying, and folding clothes, towels, sheets, etc.

If possible, **attend to the person's emotional needs**. While some people suffer from physical trauma, disability, and sickness, others deal with devastating emotional pain. Share God's Word with people suffering emotional pain. Explain how much God loves them and wants them to find healing. Suggest ways they can rest in and trust God's healing love and power. Read together with them biblical truths, discussing their meanings, and close the conversation with meaningful prayer time.

If the person has lost a loved one through illness, accident, or suicide, spend time remembering their loved one. Sometimes these conversations are difficult, but most who grieve want to remember, reflect, and talk about their lost loved ones. It helps them to heal. Be willing to listen to their stories, to share remembrances, to point out the deceased person's good traits, and explain the reasons the person will be missed. In your conversations about death, tell the person in mourning that Jesus Christ has overcome death, and that Christ brings healing peace (John 16:33).

Keep in touch (with the person who endures pain) through notes, emails, private messages, phone calls, and prearranged visits. Let them know they are not alone but loved and cared for by family and friends.

Encourage the person to talk with a counselor about his or her emotional pain. If possible, go with them, driving them, helping them find directions to the clinic, etc. If the person is a fellow church member, ask if you can invite the pastor or other church leader to visit them, talk with them, and pray with them.

Become a Wounded Healer

If you, yourself, have endured tragedy and, with God's help, have found healing, reach out to another person suffering the same type of trauma and become a wounded healer to her. What can you offer her?

QUESTIONS FOR PERSONAL REFLECTION/GROUP STUDY

You know the pain she is enduring, how discouraging her situation can be, how hopeless and helpless she may feel. You can share with her the practical ways you, yourself, found healing.

You can share with her Scriptures that helped you in your own journey of healing.

You will know the type of help she might need since you've been in her shoes and depended on help from others.

You will know how to best pray for her, what to say and what not to say. You will understand her sensitivities since you, too, encountered those who discouraged or hurt you with unintended ill-spoken or careless words.

You can show her by your example that healing is possible, and the lessons taught by pain are valuable throughout the years of one's life.

Encouraging Scriptures to Share

Perhaps you, yourself, are dealing with a painful tragedy, whether physical, emotion, mental, or spiritual. Below, we have listed some meaningful Scriptures that seek to give encouragement and hope to people undergoing crises. May you find encouragement in God's promises, and may you share them with others in need of hope and encouragement.

Sometimes in suffering, we feel alone and isolated. It seems that no one cares about us, that the pain we endure is random, serving no purpose. But **Jeremiah 29:11** helps us to know that God is still in control of our lives: "'For I know the plans I have

QUESTIONS FOR PERSONAL REFLECTION/GROUP STUDY

for you,' says the Lord. They are plans for good and not for disaster, to give you a future and a hope."

When we feel God doesn't hear our pleas, we can be assured that God does indeed hear us when we call out to Him. "Lord, you know the hopes of the helpless. Surely you will hear their cries and comfort them," the psalmist writes in **Psalm 10:17**.

When hurting people feel God has abandoned them, remind them of **Psalm 34:18**: "The Lord is close to the brokenhearted; He rescues those whose spirits are crushed."

When we hurt and no longer feel God's comfort, we can be reminded that He gives comfort. "When doubts filled my mind," wrote the psalmist in **Psalm 94:19**, "Your comfort gave me renewed hope and cheer."

When hurting people wonder if they will ever find healing, comfort them with Isaiah's powerful words: "But they that wait upon the Lord shall renew their strength; they shall mount up with wings as eagles; they shall run, and not be weary, and they shall walk, and not faint (**Isaiah 40:31**).

Remind people of God's protection through Isaiah's words: "When you go through deep waters, I will be with you. When you go through rivers of difficulty, you will not drown. When you walk through the fire of oppression, you will not be burned up; the flames will not consume you" (**Isaiah 43:2**).

Remind people of God's unfailing love in **Lamentations 3:22-24**: "The unfailing love of the Lord never ends! By His mercies, we have been kept from complete destruction. Great is His faithfulness; His mercies begin afresh each day. I say to myself, 'the Lord is my inheritance; therefore, I will hope in Him!'"

QUESTIONS FOR PERSONAL REFLECTION/GROUP STUDY

Help hurting people to understand how God might use suffering to His glory, as penned in **Romans 5:2-5**: "Through Him, we have also obtained access by faith into this grace in which we stand, and we rejoice in hope of the glory of God. More than that, we rejoice in our sufferings, knowing that suffering produces endurance, and endurance produces character, and character produces hope, and hope does not put us to shame, because God's love has been poured into our hearts through the Holy Spirit who has been given to us." (The Apostle Paul, the author of Romans, experienced incredible trauma, tragedy, and pain as a Christian in the first century. As a wounded healer, he can speak words of wisdom to those of us who suffer.)

Through Paul's words in **Romans 8:24-25**, we can encourage the suffering that they are not without hope, even if they feel hopeless: "For in this hope we were saved. Now hope that is seen is not hope. For who hopes for what he sees? But if we hope for what we do not see, we wait for it with patience." Also read to them Paul's words about hope penned in **Romans 15:4**: "For whatever was written in former days was written for our instruction, that through endurance and through the encouragement of the Scriptures we might have hope."

When hurting people suspect that their suffering will achieve no great purpose, read to them Paul's powerful words in **Romans 8:28**: "And we know that God causes everything to work together for the good of those who love God and are called according to His purpose for them."

Encourage others in pain to never lose heart nor hope by reminding them of God's promise in **2 Corinthians 4:16-18**: "Therefore we do not lose heart. Though outwardly we are wasting away, yet inwardly we are being renewed day by day.

QUESTIONS FOR PERSONAL REFLECTION/GROUP STUDY

For our light and momentary troubles are achieving for us an eternal glory that far outweighs them all. So we fix our eyes not on what is seen, but on what is unseen. For what is seen is temporary, but what is unseen is eternal."

In **Revelation 21:4**, God promises us that "He will wipe every tear from their eyes, and there will be no more death or sorrow or crying or pain. All these things are gone forever." God's promise in the book of Revelations brings us hope that pain will not last forever, and that God, Himself, will comfort us.

We can also remind those who grieve the loss of a loved one, or those who anticipate their own coming death, that death is not an end to life, but a door opened to new life in Christ. "He has caused us to be born again to a living hope through the resurrection of Jesus Christ from the dead, to an inheritance that is imperishable, undefiled, and unfading, kept in heaven for you" (**1 Peter 1:3-4**).

Additional Resources

If you are currently dealing with a tragedy or difficult situation, we have compiled a list of helpful organizations you can contact for support. Please visit DeniseGeorge.org/triumph-from-tragedy.

A Time for You to Speak

We hope that you've gained encouragement, strength, and hope as you've read the personal stories in this book. And we hope that you will share these words of wisdom, Scripture, and practical advice with others who have experienced tragedy in their lives, those who hope for healing.

QUESTIONS FOR PERSONAL REFLECTION/GROUP STUDY

We'd like to know the ways in which this volume and these stories have helped you or someone you love in their journey from sorrow and suffering to deepened faith in God and healing.

Would you please write to us and let us know what this book has meant to you? We can be reached at www.denisegeorge.org.

We will pray for you, our readers. Even though we don't know your names and needs, God knows and hears our prayers for you.

May we close this book with Paul's beautifully written benediction found in **2 Thessalonians 2:16-17**, words that remind us that God loves and comforts us in our pain and guides us in our healing:

"Now may our Lord Jesus Christ Himself and God our Father, who loved us and by His grace gave us eternal comfort and a wonderful hope, comfort you and strengthen you in every good thing you do and say."

ABOUT THE AUTHOR

Christian Writers for Life is an online community of creative Christ-followers who seek to use their God-given writing abilities to honor God and edify the world's readers. Christian Writers for Life focuses on **teaching** writers the business of writing-to-publish, **encouraging** and **supporting** writers as they hone their craft, and **celebrating** and **praying for** members as they reach out in published writing to a lost and hurting world. For more information, or to join Christian Writers for Life, visit DeniseGeorge.org.